Brini Maxwell's Guide to Gracious Living

Tips, Tricks, Recipes & Ideas to Make Your Life Bloom

Brini Maxwell's Guide to Gracious Living

Tips, Tricks, Recipes & Ideas
to Make Your Life Bloom

AS SEEN ON
style.
NETWORK

by Brini Maxwell

Photographs by Bradford Noble

Stewart, Tabori & Chang
New York

Published in 2005 by
Stewart, Tabori & Chang
115 West 18th Street
New York, NY 10011
www.abramsbooks.com

Library of Congress Cataloging-in-Publication Data
Maxwell, Brini.
    Brini Maxwell's guide to gracious living: tips, tricks, recipes, and ideas to make your life bloom/ by Brini Maxwell; photographs by Bradford Noble.
        p. cm.
    ISBN 1-58479-426-7
        1. Home economics. 2. Cookery. I. Title: Guide to gracious living. II. Title.
TX145.M35 2005
640—dc22   2005011667

Art direction and design by Tamar Cohen

The text of this book was composed in Chalet and Chalet Comprime.

Printed in China

10 9 8 7 6 5 4 3 2 1
First Printing

Stewart, Tabori & Chang is a subsidiary of

This book wouldn't have been possible without the help and support of so many. I'll try and name all of them, but please forgive me if I've forgotten any of you wonderful people. Peter and Mary Jane Sander, Amy Briamonte, Erik Nelson, William Clark, Phil Montuori, Jennifer Cohan, Dave Harding, Julie Harman, Michael Demirjian, Jeff Schwartz, Hagen Linss, Jennifer Levesque, Brad Noble, Tamar Cohen, Laura Baddish, Thom Hansen, Chad Evans, Phil Stoehr, Greg Clark, Steve Schwartz and Heather Moran, Eric Snyder, Dave Downing, Patrick McDonald, Jon Cory, Kim Cattrall, Gil Neary, Matthew Bank, Peter Hemmel, Gary Lacinski, Margaret Cho, Katie Dilks and Steve Purtee, Stephen Petracca, my wonderful crew on the television show, all the people over at E!, and most importantly, the fans, without whom I would be just another girl in New York.

Hi, people! Many of you know me from my self-titled lifestyle show on The Style Network. For those of you who don't, I'm Brini Maxwell. Since I was a child I've always been fascinated by crafting life—surroundings, experiences, alliances, anything that can be witnessed by the five senses. This has led me to explore many different disciplines, from interior design to meditation. When I started doing my television show locally in New York, little did I know it would blossom into a lovely career helping people streamline and define their lives. And since the show began airing on The Style Network in 1998, we've had so many comments and requests for more information that I just had to write a book! Some of what you'll find inside was featured on *The Brini Maxwell Show,* and some information and ideas are brand new.

What constitutes gracious living? Well, for me, it really boils down to quality of life. Many different factors compose that quality of life. Creating a lovely home that inspires me daily, represents me to my guests, and is practical, convenient, and easy to maintain; balancing the joy of eating with the responsibility of staying healthy; forming friendships and relationships that deepen and enrich my life experience; celebrating important moments with those people; and broadening my experience of the world at large are just a few. How we achieve these goals is really what defines our personality—it's the face we wear for the world. Many of us don't think much about that face, but it can be such fun to explore all the different options available. In the following pages you'll find ideas to help streamline your experience as you explore your own unique way of living. So come with me as we add style to your life and life to your style!

Now why didn't *you* think of that?

daily life

With the cacophony that is our everyday existence we often forget that this is it—we are living what we work so hard to create for ourselves. When we look at it that way, we usually realize that we've been postponing our pleasure. We think, "I'll get around to decorating my apartment someday" or "I'll just stop off at Mediocre Meals in a Hurry for dinner again tonight." Well, I say start living *now*, not in the future. Living graciously is an art, but it's one of the easy arts, not like sculpting with cross sections of animal cadavers. Here are a few ideas to give you a springboard to success.

the world we live in

Your surroundings say an awful lot about your personality. Are you Early American? Perhaps you're not that old. Are you country French? Too fussy? Maybe you—as I am—are Midcentury Modern. Whatever your style, expressing it can be an adventure in exploring yourself. Discovering your style can be fun! Immerse yourself in home furnishings—go to chain stores, thrift shops, museums, and even decorator showrooms to learn what's good, what's bad, what's out there, and what's available. Soon you'll start to see preferences emerge, and when you put them together in the same room, your unique style will be apparent. The old expression "I don't know art, but I know what I like" is an important place to start. You may not know much about what you think is pretty, but you know everything you need to know about it to invite it into your life.

Achieving your signature look can be a lot of work. Much of the work can be done yourself, such as painting, wallpapering, small construction, and sewing projects. However, you will probably find that some of what needs to be done will require working with tradesmen. This isn't something to be afraid of. The keys to a good relationship with the people you hire to work on your home are a strong sense of what you want and the ability to communicate that. For example, know the terminology they use—for upholsterers, that means terms like *welt*, *knife edge*, and *button tufting*, and for a carpenter it's phrases like *butt joint*, *dovetail*, and *piano hinge*.

The more you're able to talk their language, the closer your reality will match your vision. Remember, as with anything else, when crafting your home, Knowledge is Power!

the 4 things every room needs

provenance

The important thing when shopping for your home is not to be sucked into the belief that in order to be good a thing has to be expensive. Young people have such an edge on this, partly because of their more limited means, and partly because of their outlook. They were raised recently enough not to know that all that stuff from twenty years ago is tacky, so they're free to reinterpret it through their lens of experience and, lo and behold, it looks fresh again.

We would all do well to take a leaf out of their book when exploring what thrift shops, flea markets, and garage sales have to offer. These venues are wonderful resources for the odd and unexpected. You can buy every stick of furniture at a large chain store like Ikea or an expensive furniture store like Ethan Allen and have a beautifully turned-out room that lacks soul, but add one dented copper pot with patina or a needlepoint pillow made by someone's Aunt Minnah, and charm and personality pop.

Of course, true provenance comes from objects that have specific meaning in *your* life. Take a look at what you have in your home now, what's in your familial home's attic; examine these items with a fresh eye. When we grow up and live with things, we tend to look right through them. Consider how you would react to the item if you found it on the shelf of a thrift shop. You might just have a treasure right under your nose!

color

Most people are afraid of color. Not that they run screaming into the night if they encounter a rouge puce in a dark alley, but rather, they don't know how to use it, so they avoid it. I say color is your friend. Don't be afraid of it; welcome it into your home. There are lots of ways to do this when putting your personal space together.

Paint is without a doubt the easiest (though perhaps the messiest) way to incorporate color into a room. Many people think they have to paint all the walls in a room the same color. Personally, I think that is either bland (if you're using a pale neutral) or too much (if using a bright color). I like to use paint to direct attention. Pick a wall that you want to be the focus of attention—if it's the bedroom, the wall the bed sits against is the natural choice; if it's the living room, try the wall the entertainment center is on or the wall the davenport is against. That wall should be painted your accent color. The other walls should be painted a coordinating neutral. This technique can also be used with wallpaper. It can be an economical way to use expensive paper and still enjoy the effect it creates. Notice how the orange wall in the illustration (opposite) draws attention to the art displayed on it. Imagine how the room would look if that wall had been painted the same color as the others—boring, huh? And so many people ignore the ceiling, the forgotten fifth wall. It can be the perfect canvas for expressing your own personal sense of color. They think that painting the ceiling a dark color will visually lower it. This may or may not be true, depending on your architecture, but it can also create a cozy, intimate feeling and, like rugs and different floor surfaces in the same space, it can help to define different spaces in your room.

Color can also be incorporated into a room with fabrics—upholstered furniture, drapery, and wall upholstery can brighten things immeasurably. Imagine how dull an all-neutral room with all-neutral furniture would look, then imagine the same room with furniture that contrasts with the colors of the walls—chocolate brown sofa and chairs with pale blue walls and an ecru drape across one wall, perhaps.

Lastly, accent pieces can provide pops of complementary color. Try using an orange vase in a blue room or a red pillow on a brown divan. Those unexpected touches are the ones that make you smile.

grandeur

Most rooms have the potential for drama. What grandeur usually boils down to is scale. Sometimes that comes from proportion—a high ceiling or long, low room, when maximized with color, furniture placement, and lighting, can be all the drama you need. If your proportions are more ordinary, you can bring drama into a room by playing with scale in several different ways. Big patterns can be as frightening as color. They can also, however, be a wonderful way to create interest and express your larger-than-life personality.

The scale of a pattern and how it relates to the surface it's applied to can be the basis of a very playful room. Try using an enormous, patterned fabric as upholstery on a piece of accent furniture or as curtains. Or paint a graphic on a wall that's been enlarged enough to expand beyond the boundaries of the wall it's applied to. It can continue on to the next surface, like in the illustration (opposite) or end at the corner. This sort of treatment is called a supergraphic and is used to great effect in small rooms.

Scale can also be employed to great advantage in choice of furnishings. A long sofa can be extremely effective on a long wall; an enormous headboard or wardrobe can give a room a focal point. Similarly, art can be used to create a

sense of drama. When I say this, I'm speaking of a broader interpretation of art—
if it's visually interesting, it can be featured as art. The Shakers hung chairs on the
wall. This idea can be reinterpreted with today's esthetics in mind by mounting
other furniture on the wall rather than placing it on the floor. Massing is perhaps
the easiest way to give your room some pizzazz with grandeur. Collectors have a
head start on massing; put all your objects together on shelves on one wall and
you have instant drama. Grandeur is what makes a room special. It brings out the
diva in your surroundings.

nature

Rooms should breathe. You don't want the only living thing in your room to be you. Exploring the world of horticulture is a very satisfying endeavor. Whether it's herbs on the kitchen windowsill, ferns in the bathroom, or forced bulbs in the living room, plants are a joy and add another dimension to a beautiful home. Even if you don't have a green thumb, you can still have that touch of life in your home. Plants don't have to live forever; they can be like cut flowers—you can replace them when they get weedy or start to turn brown. I like to keep a planter in my living room and swap out its contents when the whim suits me, perhaps when I'm entertaining or the seasons are changing. You wouldn't keep poinsettias or forced bulbs around as they're dying, so if your fern takes a nose-dive and won't revive, replace it!

Watering houseplants needn't be a chore. You can water your hanging plants with ice cubes so the water doesn't run through as quickly and make a mess below the plant. If you're going away, coil a piece of cotton rope (it must be cotton) around the base of your houseplant's soil and secure it with large hairpins. Then put the other end in a glass of water. The water will wick up the cotton and keep your plant watered until you get home. As for food for your lit-tle green friends, crushed eggshells and coffee grounds make wonderful plant fertilizer.

feather your nest — and keep it preened!

paint your life easy

The basic tools and supplies for achieving professional quality results when painting are good brushes and rollers and quality paint. Paint the baseboards and crown moldings in semigloss and the walls in flat or eggshell (except in the bathroom and kitchen, which should all get at least semigloss or enamel). When applying the paint, roll it on in an M pattern and then cross it horizontally. Aside from that, here are some more esoteric painting tips to help make a professional job easier to acquire.

➼ Hate getting little dots of paint on your hardware? Rub a little petroleum jelly on the hinges of your doors before painting them; flecks and spots will wipe off easily.

➤ Getting paint on the rim of your paint can makes such a mess. It runs down the sides, leaving spots on the drop cloth that get stepped in and tracked all over the house, bringing back unpleasant guilty feelings about tracking mud on your mother's newly scrubbed linoleum. Put a large rubber band vertically around the can, so that it stretches across the opening, then use that, rather than the rim of the can, to wipe the excess paint from your brush. You'll save paint, the can won't be so untidy when you're finished, and your therapy sessions will be much more tranquil.

→ If you want to take a break from painting but don't have time to clean out

your brushes and rollers, wrap them in plastic wrap and put them in the fridge. When you're ready to resume they'll be fresh as toast.

➡ Chandeliers have enough to worry about with fly specks. Keep them from getting paint specks by covering them with those thin plastic bags you get from the dry cleaner.

➡ Another thing you can do with those dry cleaner bags is use them as painting smocks. Cut holes for head and arms and reinforce the cut edges with tape. However, do be careful putting them on and taking them off. Our goal is a beautiful paint job, not asphyxiation.

➤ Those pesky paint splatters, much like that nail color that was such a mistake, can be easily cleaned from glass and formica with nail polish remover. Use a cotton ball or even just a folded-up paper towel and wipe away. Avoid using it on plastic, varnished wood, and painted surfaces, however.

➡ If you have only a small amount of paint left after painting a room, transfer it to a small glass jar and save it for touch-ups later.

light up your life

Lighting is so important. It makes us look beautiful and see beautifully. We wouldn't want to live our whole lives in task lighting, nor would we want to perform tasks by candlelight. My friend, lighting designer Randy Wilson, says there are four basic aspects to consider when planning any lighting scheme.

➡ Esthetics: How does your lighting make the room—and you—look?

➡ Performance: What are the operational and practical considerations of the light sources?

➡ Function: How does the lighting address the needs in your room?

➡ Position: From where in the room does the lighting come?

When designing the lighting for a living room, you might value esthetics over function and performance; when designing the lighting for a kitchen, function might be your primary concern; and for a garage, your needs might run more toward performance. Randy also suggests that when planning out your room you make allowances for the different activities that might take place there. For example, don't put your overhead fixtures and your lamps on the same switch—you won't be able to vary the quality of light in your room enough for, say, cleaning and entertaining.

Speaking of switches, one of the most important tools of the lighting designer is a dimmer. They can be easily installed for incandescent fixtures by a layperson and will make your rooms so much more habitable (fluorescent dimmers should be installed by an electrician). Find the dimmer style you'd like (there are many to choose from) and follow the directions on the package for installation.

Candles are a lovely way to create soft accent lighting. Here are a few things to think about, however, when using them: Candles should not be kept in drafts. That's what makes them drip. Place them in still areas, not near open windows, fans, or air conditioners. You can keep the cleanup time down by using drip guards at the base of tapers. These inexpensive glass disks fit over candle holders and catch those drips before they cause havoc with your holders and tabletops. They can be found in a variety of styles and patterns. Candles will burn longer if you store them in the freezer or soak them in soapsuds before burning them (being careful not to saturate the wick).

Your candlesticks (especially the ornate ones) can be a problem to keep clean. There is a simple way to do this, however. Place your waxy candlestick on top of a brown paper bag in your oven, and set it at its lowest heat. The wax will melt off and soak into the paper. The melted wax will also evenly coat your candlestick, creating a lovely finish that will protect the candlestick from tarnish. I've done this with some wooden Danish modern candlesticks; they came out with a beautiful satiny finish on them that cooled to a hard protective coating. In addition, you'll find that the wax-saturated paper makes wonderful kindling for your fireplace.

The lovely glow of candles can create yet another problem; what to do should wax drip on your furniture? Scraping the wax off can leave ugly scratches. Unfortunately, it's the best way to remove colored wax. Scraping will be easier if you harden the wax by putting an ice cube on it. Use your fingers for the initial removal and then, rather than using a knife or other metal object, try a plastic scraper or spatula—even a credit card will work in a pinch. Finish with a little furniture polish. White wax is a much easier problem to solve. Take out another brown paper bag and get your iron. Put the bag over the wax and, with the iron on the lowest heat, pass it over the bag, repositioning the brown paper until the wax has all been absorbed. This method can also be used on carpeting and fabric. Don't try this with colored wax, though; the dyes are apt to stain.

love your walls— they'll love you back!

Wallpaper needn't look shabby when you know how to patch. It's really very simple. The secret is not to cut the patch out. It will blend in almost invisibly if you tear the patch out, being careful to tear away from the front so you're left with edges that bevel from back to front. The edges are very thin and blend in well with the existing paper on the wall. Match the area to be repaired to your extra wallpaper and tear out a patch large enough to cover the hole with approximately one inch extra around the edges. Apply the patch with wallpaper paste or white glue and smooth out with a flat ruler. Sponge off any excess glue and let dry. This process can be used not only for tears and holes, but also for stains and scuff marks. If the stain is an oil stain, treat it first with cornstarch or flour to pull the oil out so it doesn't seep through.

Of course, in order to patch you must have saved what was left of the roll when the initial job was finished. And the process works best with paper wall covering, rather than vinyl, which doesn't tear and must be cut. For painted walls, pick up a few extra paint chips in the color of your choice. The small pieces of paper can be used to patch holes. They'll match the color of the wall exactly. Here's a tip from the photography industry: When you paint your walls, paint a few strips of masking tape at the same time. They can be used to cover cracks and holes in the wall after the paint job is finished.

You might also want to take this opportunity to shield your corners with corner guards—clear plastic corner strips that are about one inch wide on either face and usually have clear adhesive strips already in them for easy mounting. They will make sure your corners are ever lovely. With a little care and forethought, you need never have dog-eared walls.

keeping it clean

Cleaning your home can be such a chore, but it doesn't have to be. In my travels I've discovered some clever little tricks that help make the oftentimes unpleasant task of home maintenance, if not a joy, then at least a little less tiresome. Here are some of my favorites.

A room that needs to be cleaned can sometimes be a trifle overwhelming—sometimes so much so that we end up procrastinating until the minister is due for dinner and it absolutely *has* to be done this instant. A simple solution for avoiding that stress is to tackle it regularly and think of your room as a big clock. Start at twelve o'clock and work your way back around to twelve o'clock again. If you focus on one area (hour) at a time, you'll find that you aren't so put off by the whole task. You'll also be able to "stop the clock" at will and return to it later without being discombobulated.

How many times have we looked at our **can opener** and wondered what the gunk was in the gears? The detritus of a thousand cans of everything, from cream of spinach soup to cat food, doesn't make an appetizing start to a tuna salad sandwich. The solution is a pipe cleaner. It can be used to clean those messy gears—and makes for less quease with great ease.

How dull is the task of cleaning your **toilet**? You can keep all that's vitreous virtuous by dropping a fizzy denture tablet in the bowl. Don't scrub—effervesce your way to sparkling porcelain!

A Chopin nocturne deserves the best, so if your **piano** looks like it's been

wood maintenance
it's not just about dusting, you know!

Dust is the bane of carved furniture's existence, and it tends to make one's home look a little like Miss Havisham's. There is, however, a simple solution. Instead of using a cloth on it, try a soft pastry brush or even a Q-Tip with a bit of furniture polish on it. Use that with a cloth to catch drips and remove excess polish. Your precious heirloom will look brand-new.

Another wonderful suggestion for polishing your wood furniture is to sprinkle on a little cornstarch after the initial application of polish, then buff to a high gloss. The cornstarch absorbs the oil and leaves a lovely, fingerprint-free shine.

If you find yourself with a white ring on one of your tables, there is a simple way to remove it: Rub the ring with mayonnaise—it will magically disappear.

Have you ever had a piece of paper stick to a varnished surface? Here's a solution: Pour olive oil on the paper, drop by drop, and rub it in with a cloth. Repeat until you can gently lift the paper away.

enjoying too much coffee and red wine, don't call in the family dentist. Just use a pink pet eraser to clean those less than white keys, and your piano will smile unselfconsciously again.

Most people will agree that smoking is a filthy habit. However, it does have its upside. Cigarette ashes make an excellent **silver or gold polish** when mixed with water to make a smooth paste. Your jewelry will sparkle beautifully on those yellow fingers!

If you have a **clutter problem**, pick a spot in the middle of the room—it could be your coffee table or even your davenport—and take everything that doesn't belong on the surfaces of your room and put it all in that one spot. It's much easier to ferry the items back to their homes if you take them out of their comfort zones in the corners and on the counters of your room.

Now, many of you have white sinks in your homes. They look lovely . . . until they get stained. There's a quick fix for that. Before you go to bed, line the sink with paper towels and saturate the towels with everyday household bleach. When you get up and remove the towels, your sink will sparkle like new!

Those ugly **brown stains on dishes** left by cigarettes can be easily removed with a cork and ordinary table salt. Moisten the salt and dip the cork in it, then rub the spot with the salt. The stain will disappear like magic.

Lighter fluid is a wonderful cleaning solvent. Use it to eliminate **skid marks** from your kitchen floor, stubborn stickers from glassware, and otherwise recalcitrant **smudges** from countertops. It also removes rust spots from stainless steel appliances, sinks, and countertops, will unstick stamps from an envelope if you saturate them from the back, and will lift oil-based stains like lipstick from your carpet if the stain is first treated with a few drops of glycerin. It will lift paint and varnish slightly, so it's best not to use it on those surfaces. I strongly suggest not lighting up when cleaning with lighter fluid. We don't like singed eyebrows, now, do we?

Speaking of **carpets**, they can be spot-cleaned with the suds of a mild detergent, such as dishwashing liquid. Remembering to use only the suds, apply with a sponge to the affected area. For a general light carpet cleaning, sprinkle the entire floor with baking soda, leave it for about thirty minutes, and vacuum. To eliminate odors, leave the baking soda on overnight. Grease spots can be removed by mounding cornstarch onto the stain immediately. Let stand for at least twelve hours, vacuum up, and repeat if necessary. Soft area rugs can be helpful in keeping floors clean. Put them in high traffic areas, and when they get dirty toss them in the washing machine.

Wearing **high heels** improves balance and strengthens muscles not other-wise used as much. Why not multitask and wear your Manolos when you waltz around with the vacuum? Be careful, through. Wearing heels too often can shorten your Achilles tendon, so I suggest dusting in flats.

Stoves and ovens can be a chore to keep clean. Here are some ideas for making the job easier:

➡ Soak those reflectors in some hot soapy water for a while and they'll come clean. Or, if they're enameled, try a solution of hot water and baking soda. After they've soaked a bit, scrub them with a scouring pad—they'll sparkle like new.

➤ Now, if you're like me, you probably want to keep the reflectors looking fresh and clean. This can be accomplished by wrapping them in aluminum foil. After fitting the foil into the depression and around the edges, cut a star into the center hole and wrap around there, too. When the bowls get dirty, simply replace it. You can save yourself even more work by covering the unused burners with tin pie plates while cooking.

➡➡ If your gas jets are burning unevenly, try cleaning the ports with something like a pipe cleaner or unbent paper clip. Don't, however, use a toothpick or some other item that might break off in the port, thereby nullifying your original purpose.

➡ If you're baking a pie, put the pie plate on a cookie or jelly roll sheet with a raised edge. It will catch any drips and keep your oven floor clean. Another tip for keeping your oven floor clean: Line it with aluminum foil when baking messy dishes. I recommend replacing the foil with each dish rather than waiting for it to get very dirty. We don't like messy tin foil cluttering up our oven, now, do we?

➡➡ Commercial oven cleaners are effective but very caustic; use them with care and follow all the instructions on the can. Cover the floor in front of the oven with newspaper, wear rubber gloves, and keep your wits about you. If your oven is electric, you can use ammonia to get at that dirt. (Don't try this with gas ovens—the combination of ammonia and gas fumes can make for an explosive situation.) Put a small bowl of ammonia in the oven and leave it overnight. In the morning, scrub the oven with a bucket of water with one cup of ammonia in it. Again, newspaper and rubber gloves are the order of the day.

who are you? (in the larger sense, not just...well...you know what i mean)

Developing a sense of style is all about being objective. It's difficult to get the ego out of the way when confronting our image in the mirror, but it's essential if we're going to be our best self. Whether you accept yourself as you are or want to change some things, what's important is to acknowledge them. Once we do that we can then start to explore what works in terms of clothing, hairstyles, and makeup.

When shopping for clothing, you usually try it on in a dressing room with only one mirror. Keep in mind, though, that people will see you from all angles, not just the front. It's a good idea to have a small mirror handy so you can check out some of those other angles. Try to regard the image in the mirror as if it is someone else entirely—would you respond positively to what you see, or would the clothing (not the person, remember) inspire an uncharitable comment? Many stores offer alteration services; take advantage of them. It's in the stores' best interest for you to look your best in their clothing.

Hairstyles are a similar proposition. I suggest spending some money on this initially. It's an investment. If you see someone with a particularly becoming hairstyle that represents the type of person you see yourself as (just because a mullet is particularly well executed is no reason to patronize that stylist expecting to get the perfect Rachel), ask the name of his or her stylist.

As far as makeup is concerned, less is more—it should be generally noticed for its absence. It is fine to highlight a certain area of your face, but pick *one*—eyes, mouth, *or* cheeks, not eyes, mouth, *and* cheeks.

gifts we give ourselves

pets

People are not solitary animals. We're designed to commune with other animals, both human and nonhuman. Welcoming a pet into your life can be such a joy. It's been proven that elderly people who have pets are healthier and happier than those who don't. I think that's because having another wonderful little creature around gives us an outlet for love. The more love we express, the better we feel about life. I like most animals, but I especially like cats. Some people say they're haughty and aloof. They can be, but few who have had a purring cat fall asleep on their lap or seen a cat "smile" when chucked under the chin can maintain their prejudice for long. When adopting an animal, it's important to act responsibly. Unless you intend to breed it, have it spayed or neutered. The irresponsible proliferation of animals and their subsequent abandonment amounts to cruelty. If you want to, you can find people who will help you acclimate your animal to home life. I discovered that my physical trainer is one such person. He's an enormous body builder who dotes on kittens. Clarence encourages them to use their litter box and knows how to start them off on the right track with house manners, like not scratching the furniture or climbing the drapes (or the pet owner). Once an animal is ensconced in your home, your life will never be the same.

hobbies

Finding time to explore something interesting isn't always easy, but doing just that can make life mean so much more. One of my hobbies is needlework. It's perfect for my hectic life, and I find it a good way to keep my hands busy when spending time with friends, watching TV, or flying hither and yon, as I seem to be doing more often lately. This and other multitasking hobbies like knitting are wonderful because you have something to show for them periodically when you finish projects.

I also enjoy collecting; it has become something of an obsession. I collect many different things, all with the common thread of having come from the '50s, '60s, or '70s. Finding something to occupy your time can act as a pressure-release valve, making you a more balanced, grounded person.

hot bubble baths

A hot bath is like a warm hug. What makes a bubble bath so delightful? It releases all the tension of the day and can relax you to the point of stupor, if you want it to. Holistic healing suggests that hot baths induce an artificial fever, which can help you conquer infection by killing off the infectants in your system and bringing toxins in the body to the surface to be flushed away by perspiration. The warm water, with its soothing bubbles and the fresh smell of lavender (or whatever fragrance you prefer), even the quality of light in the room, can contribute to your rejuvenation.

Let's talk about making those bubbles. There are many products out there to create mountains of bubbles to immerse yourself in, but why not do it economically?

false eyelashes

False eyelashes can add such glamour to your look. I use Vogue brand number 210; they look lush and natural in brown. Using false eyelashes needn't be an occasional thing. Why not make them part of your everyday look? There are all sorts available, from wild and unreal to natural styles suitable for everyday wear. They're simple to apply. Put a thin bead of glue along the strip of the lash (I like to use an applicator of some sort–the handle end of a lip brush, for example) and then position the lash as close to your natural lash line as you can. It's a good idea to curl your own lashes and apply a touch of mascara before applying the false lashes. Applying the mascara after you've applied the lash can make them too caked, and the cleaner you keep them the longer they'll last.

We all have those small pieces of soap left after wearing down a bar. They're difficult to wash up with and rather a nuisance to have around. Collect them in a small mesh bag and tie them under your tub's spigot. The water running through them will create lovely bubbles for pennies a bath.

If you'd like to take that bath to the next level, why not try a whirlpool spa? You don't need to go out and buy a new bathtub. Models are available that fit over the edge of your existing tub and make lovely bubbles to melt your worries away.

make your mornings more mellifluous

What side of bed do you get up on? Are your mornings rushed? Are you a Gloomy Gus because you don't have enough time? Well, here are some ideas that will help.

Try **planning your mornings** out the night before. So many things can be done before you go to bed to streamline matters. Start by deciding what you'll wear. Laying out your clothes the night before will do away with muffle-headed waffling in the morning. Showering the night before is also a time-saver.

Another thing that makes mornings easier is setting up **breakfast beforehand**. Lay out your place setting and put the cereal in the bowl (not the milk, of course). Set up the necessary ingredients for your smoothie and your morning will be that much simpler.

Let's talk a little about **ways to wake up**. Conventional alarm clocks can be so jarring; so can news radio, with its depressing running commentary on the ills of society. Why not start your day with something gentler, like jazz or classical? Something light is lovely. You can get alarm clocks with CD players in them now, which are perfect for waking up to your own tune. Another way to wake up that's sort of fun is to call a restaurant the night before for breakfast delivery. Just imagine waking up to hot coffee and a muffin or sweet roll.

Good humor in the morning means a happy, productive day and, consequently, a happier and more productive world. So, remember: the difference between world peace and all hell breaking loose comes down to your morning routine. I'm sure you'll buckle down, do your part, and know the world thanks you.

laundry

We are what we wear, so it's important to keep tidy. However, nobody likes doing laundry, except maybe my producer Julie, who finds it therapeutic. But it is a necessary task for maintaining a fresh appearance. Here are a few ideas to make the job a little less loathsome.

Stains should be attacked right after they occur. Oil and grease stains should be covered with a mound of flour or cornstarch and left for a few days to allow the powder to suck the offending stain out of the cloth; red wine can be neutralized with white wine or absorbed by salt; other stains, such as chocolate, cranberry juice, and fresh blood, benefit from a touch of seltzer (it's not a cocktail I'd recommend for anyone other than, perhaps, a vampire). When washing the stained clothes, a pretreater will help with the stain removal. Above all, if the stain doesn't come out in the first wash, don't put the garment in the dryer or, heaven forbid, iron it! That will just set the stain. Rewash it using the same process.

We all hate the WHABUMP of an **unbalanced load** in the washing machine. If this occurs more often than it should, try leveling your machine. There are little leveling knobs on the bottom that you can use to raise the washer by turning them to the left or lower it by turning them to the right. If you don't have a level, a measuring cup will work just as well. Fill it to any line and set it on top of the washer. When the water in it is at the line all the way around the cup, the washer is level.

Ironing is a bore (except for Julie)—there are so many other things to be doing. But it's a necessary chore, unless you're going for that world-weary, rumpled-traveler look. When ironing cottons and linens, use a spray bottle; the dampness will help release the wrinkles and the shirt will look that much crisper. You can also put a few drops of your favorite perfume in the steam chamber of your iron, and your pressed dainties will emanate the lovely smell. By the way, if clothes are taken out of the drier immediately after it stops, they will be much fresher and might not need ironing at all.

Tired of **ring-around-the-collar**? Treat the stain with a little shampoo applied with a toothbrush; rub it in well—it's made to dissolve body oils—and then wash as usual. That ring will disappear like a husband on trash day.

daily bread

The old adage "you are what you eat" is true not only in a physical way, but a philosophical one as well. If our diet consists of bland, boring fare with no imagination and we explore our gastronomic desires only on special occasions, then we cheat ourselves out of one of the joys of life. Of course, it's important to be responsible eaters and not overindulge the id (as Freud would call it). What's worked for me is to find an everyday diet that allows me to eat most of what I like without gaining weight. I keep only what's on my diet in my home for day-to-day eating. In my case, this includes cold cuts, whole milk, and Metracal. I'm not a food Nazi, however. I eat what I like, whether it's on my diet or not, when I'm at a party (it's bad manners to present your host or hostess with dietary restrictions that are not medically based when invited to their home) or a restaurant. This system of responsible self-indulgence allows me to keep my figure while still enjoying the wonderful bounty life has to offer. Making basic fare fabulous is easy when you use your imagination. The key to "easy" is not being averse to using ready-made ingredients and time-saving devices. The recipes I've assembled in this chapter are designed to make nutritious eating fun and easy.

breakfast

Getting a proper start to the day is extremely important. Here are some quick breakfast dishes to get you off on the right foot:

Smoothies are a great way to start your day in the pink! And they're so easy to make in your blender. Because they are the entire fruit blended up, they can be a complete vegetarian breakfast. You can add soy protein, deodorized garlic, or even cayenne pepper if you have a cold. On the side of culinary delectability, try frozen yogurt, ice cream, or honey. Keep the berries in the freezer. They make your smoothie ice-cold without having to add ice.

banana-strawberry smoothie

Though bananas give this smoothie its base, you don't need to use them—or strawberries either. The possibilities are truly endless. Try combinations of blueberries, pineapple, papaya, mango, and juices like orange, cranberry, pear nectar, or grape. They really bring out your innate creativity. Once you've mastered your favorite, why not branch out into vegetable smoothies? Just imagine avocado and olive!

You'll need:

> *½ large banana*
> *4 strawberries*
> *1 cup apple juice*

Cut up the banana, wash and hull the strawberries, and put both in your blender. Add the apple juice and blend until smooth (hence the name "smoothie").

Serves 1

the one-dish breakfast—a meal that multitasks

This dish is wonderful for us girls on the go. It's a complete meal in one pan: hot, nutritious, satisfying, and perfect for a family.

You'll need:

> 2 cups biscuit dough from mix, prepared according to package instructions
> 8 strips bacon, cooked to just under perfection and blotted with paper towels
> 1 cup milk
> 4 eggs, beaten
> 2 cups light cream
> 1/2 teaspoon pepper
> 1 1/4 cups grated Swiss cheese
> 2 cups grated cheddar cheese

Preheat oven to 350°F. Spread the biscuit dough in a greased 9-by-13-inch baking dish, then lay the bacon out over it. Mix up the rest of the ingredients and pour the mixture over the biscuit dough and bacon. Bake for 1 hour, until golden brown. Cut into squares and serve.

Serves 6

lunch

Carrying our lunch to work, or "brown bagging" it, is an American tradition as sacrosanct as saluting the flag. You're sure of the food's nutritional value and it's a less expensive alternative to buying your lunch. Your parcel of choice doesn't have to be a brown bag, however. Nowadays, there are so many other more attractive and well-planned-out options—clever little boxes with compartments and spill-proof lids, insulated nylon sacks, and even vintage or vintage-inspired lunch boxes are splendid solutions to the boxed lunch problem. And when it comes to soup, there's nothing like a Thermos. The insulated container with its little cap that doubles as a cup is a delightful design coup.

Of course, you may not work at a job where carrying your lunch is necessary. Whatever your mid-day meal circumstances, making sure your lunch is well balanced is very important. Soup is the perfect portable dish. It's easy to transport, reheats well, and provides you with all the energy needed to finish up your day. The soup recipes that follow can be the base for a nutritious lunch, but you'll want to round out your meal with a salad or sandwich, fruit juice or water, and if you like, a little treat of some kind like a cookie or brownie to perk up your afternoon.

marvelous matzoh balls

Matzoh balls are delicious, warm, and inviting in soup, which is just great if you're not feeling well—it's so important to maintain proper nutrition when you're sick, and this is the original cold remedy. If it's good enough for a Jewish mother, it's good enough for you.

The important thing about matzoh balls is that they are good and hard— they should be like little rocks. This can be achieved with *gänzeschmalz* (Yiddish for goose fat); you can also use chicken fat. Now, some of you may be wondering where on God's green earth you're going to find this. It can be obtained at markets in Jewish neighborhoods, or you can render it yourself the next time you fix a chicken: Just cut the fat away from the meat, put it in a frying pan, and gently heat it until it melts.

You can use homemade stock or canned broth or even use the matzoh balls to perk up canned chicken noodle soup. I guarantee this will cure whatever ails you.

You'll need:

> *1 tablespoon gänzeschmalz*
> *1 egg*
> *¼ cup matzoh meal*
> *1 dash each salt, pepper, and nutmeg*
> *4 cups good-quality chicken broth*

Combine all the ingredients well in a small bowl and chill for a little while in the fridge. Form into small balls. Cook the balls in your lovely chicken broth, heated to a simmer, until they float to the surface.

Makes 8 small balls; serves 2–4

asparagus soup — sometimes love is green

Vegetable-based soups are wonderful because they're light and refreshing but also filling. This asparagus soup recipe is my father's. It's really wonderful for two reasons: It's tasty and good for you. Instead of using cream or milk, you thicken it with potatoes—much healthier. If you'd like a richer soup, you can substitute raw avocados for asparagus; for a lighter soup, try raw cucumber. This soup is perfect for the lunch pail because it's good cold. But be sure to bring extra. The people sitting next to you will surely want you to share!

You'll need:

2 pounds asparagus
¼ cup olive oil or margarine
1 cup diced potatoes
4 whole scallions, chopped
4 cups chicken broth
2–3 tablespoons chopped fresh dill
2 teaspoons white wine Worcestershire sauce
Freshly ground white pepper to taste
Salt, to taste

Break off and discard the white, fibrous ends of the asparagus. Cut the spears into 1-inch lengths. In a soup pot over a medium heat, heat the oil and sauté the potatoes, scallions, and asparagus for 3 minutes. Add the broth, dill, Worcestershire, and pepper. Simmer until the vegetables are tender, about 30 minutes, then reserve several asparagus tips for garnish. Puree the mixture in 2 or 3 batches in your blender or food processor. Return to the pot and heat until steaming, but do not boil. Add salt to taste.

Serves 6

dinner

Din-din needn't be a complicated affair in order to be inspiring. Try these simple ideas to make your evening meals sparkle.

the humble burger

Hamburgers and turkey burgers are staples of the American food landscape. But they can sometimes be bland. Here are some ways to make them interesting again:

➡ Try a pesto burger. The simple addition of pesto sauce (either homemade or store-bought) will add delightfully unexpected flavor.

➡ If you find turkey burgers dry but like the lower fat content, try adding mushrooms. They release moisture when cooked, which will keep your burgers from drying out as they cook.

➡ The standard for improving burgers is onion soup mix. Just blend a packet in with your ground meat before forming it into patties. You can also use other soup mixes to improve your burgers—though avoid the ones with noodles.

Casseroles

Casseroles are an easy way to keep food at your finger-tips, ready to serve in a trice. In fact, you can make casseroles in advance and you'll have an entire week's worth of meals all set for those busy times of the year. Just assemble the casserole in the baking dish, lined with heavyweight plastic wrap (be sure to press the wrap down flatly into the dish). Instead of baking, pop the dish into the freezer, then when the casserole is frozen, turn it out of the dish and store it in the freezer until you need it. When you're ready, just unwrap it, pop it back into the dish, defrost, and bake as directed. A frozen casserole is also a wonderful gift for a new mother, and also a thoughtful mit-bring for someone sitting shiva.

janet leigh's meat loaf—don't eat this in the shower!

We would hardly be giving ground meat its due without mentioning meat loaf. Here's a favorite recipe that originated with Janet Leigh—I'm sure there were many evenings when this delicious dish found its way from her kitchen to the table, to the delight of Tony and little Jamie Lee.

You'll need:

> *3 pounds ground veal or very lean beef*
> *1 pound ground pork*
> *1/2 cup minced onion*
> *4 carrots, grated*
> *1 tablespoon salt*
> *1/4 teaspoon pepper*
> *1/2 cup sour cream*

Preheat the oven to 350°F. Combine all the ingredients and pack the mixture into a 9-by-5-inch loaf pan. Bake for 90 minutes. What could be easier than that?

Serves 4

crown roast of cheese

This is delicious with a salad and a good Chardonnay or Pinot Grigio.

You'll need:

> *1/4 cup (1/2 stick) butter*
> *Seven 1/2-inch-thick slices bread (sourdough is nice, but any kind will do)*
> *1 cup grated sharp cheddar cheese*
> *2 eggs*
> *1 cup milk*
> *1 teaspoon salt*
> *1/4 teaspoon paprika*
> *Pinch of cayenne*
> *1/2 teaspoon dry mustard*

Preheat the oven to 350°F and grease your 3- or 4-quart casserole dish (butter will do nicely). Butter all slices of bread on both sides. Cut two slices twice on the bias (from corner to corner), creating eight triangles—set these aside. Cube the remaining bread (there should be about 4 cups). Layer the bread cubes in your buttered casserole dish alternately with the grated cheese until you've run out of both cheese and bread. In a small bowl, beat the remaining ingredients together and pour over the casserole, then place the triangles of bread around the edge, forming a crown. Bake for 25 minutes and serve immediately.

Serves 4 as a main dish, 6 as a side

gourmet mac & cheese — a gift from the cheese gods

This is the best macaroni and cheese in the world. And it's lots of fun to make, to boot. The recipe was given to me by Jesse Ramos, a wonderful chef, who appeared on my show to demonstrate how to make it.

You'll need:

1 pound farfalle pasta
1/2 cup (1 stick) butter
2 shallots, minced
6 tablespoons all-purpose flour
1 1/2 teaspoons dry mustard
1/8 teaspoon cayenne
4 cups buttermilk
3 cups (about 12 ounces) coarsely grated extra-sharp white cheddar cheese
1 1/3 cups freshly grated Parmesan cheese
Fresh seasoned bread crumbs

Preheat oven to 350°F and butter a 3- or 4-quart casserole dish. Boil the pasta until just al dente (about 7 minutes), drain well, put in a large bowl, and set aside. In a heavy saucepan, melt 7 tablespoons of the butter over medium-low heat. Add the shallots and cook until transparent. Add flour to make a roux, whisking for 3 minutes, then add the mustard and cayenne and whisk well. Add the buttermilk in four parts, whisking in between. Bring to a boil and cook until thickened, whisking occasionally. Pour the sauce over the pasta, then add the cheddar and 1 cup of the Parmesan and mix well. Pour the mixture into the casserole dish. In a small bowl, combine the bread crumbs and the remaining Parmesan, then sprinkle the mixture over the pasta. Cut up the remaining 1 tablespoon butter and dot the top with it. Pop the casserole into the oven for 30 to 40 minutes, or until golden brown and bubbling. Serve with a green salad for roughage.

Serves 6 as a main dish, 8 as a side

entertaining

The most important thing I can say about entertaining is *relax*. So many people are petrified at the mere notion of hosting an affair. When you think of it as bringing a group of friends together to enjoy each other's company, your fear will implode like a collapsed soufflé. If you're comfortable and at ease, your guests will be too. Throwing wonderful parties is easy if you give them a little thought. Assemble a group of amicable people, present them with delicious food and tempting libations, and your party will be a resounding success.

getting ready

Entertaining is scary only if you feel unprepared. If you've dotted your i's and crossed your t's, there's no reason to be nervous. Planning your party can be fun, kind of like assembling a crazy quilt: a compatible group of eccentric people, aural and visual stimulation, delightful diversions, and, of course, a reason for gathering everyone—even if that reason is no reason at all. In the next few pages you'll find everything you need to assemble the quilt of many colors that is a successful fête.

the alchemy of the guest list

Most of us know an awful lot of people and it would be impractical to invite everyone to our homes every time we have an affair. Plus, it is important to find the right balance of personalities. For large cocktail parties, this is less of an issue than at smaller gatherings. For those intimate fêtes, it's important to consider what your guests have in common. Certain combinations can be as volatile as nitroglycerine—and we don't want any carnage, now, do we? Perhaps you have a friend who works in law enforcement. It's probably not the best idea to seat him next to your friend the grifter. For that matter, you might want to exclude one of that pair from your guest list for this particular party altogether. Instead, why not invite that nice man you met who works for the CIA? Your policeman friend will be fascinated to hear how things are done at the "Agency." When you introduce them, be sure to start the conversation going in that direction. Other combinations to avoid are rabid political party members, warring coworkers (it's probably best to avoid inviting either of them, lest the one not invit-ed gets wind of it and thinks you're playing favorites; perhaps if they're both not invited and find out why, it might make them see how their war has affected their own lives), animal trainers and animal-rights activists, and divorced or sep-arated couples (invite the one you feel closest to if you must invite one of them).

The role of a hostess is to foster new friendships among her guests. It's impor-tant, therefore, to consider who your guests are, their interests, backgrounds, and quirks, and to find connections between them and point them out in conversation. Have a few conversation starters around to keep things moving if you encounter lulls. On my coffee table I have an electric match. It's a black plastic ball with a small handle on the top sitting on a foot. When you pull out the handle it ignites a wick on the end so you can light your cigarette. This is an object of endless fascination for guests, especially when conversation lags. Once you master the art of human mixology and conversational creativity, you'll find that your parties take on a life of their own and you'll be known as a great host or hostess.

music

Music can be as important as your guest list. I like to curate my music collection and assemble the perfect mix for each occasion. It's so easy these days to do this with MP3s and music-playing programs. I create a CD of wonderful cocktail music to keep the party rolling along. One of the types of music I find useful when enter-taining is instrumentals. It doesn't intrude on the conversation and the unfamiliar pieces can be made into a subject of conversation, should there be a lack of something to discuss. If you're feeling ambitious, explore the world of production, or library music. This music is created as background tracks for film and television, and you can find collections of it from the '50s, '60s, and '70s. It's almost always instrumental, and when it comes from the periods mentioned above, it's all acoustic and usually played by talented musicians. I've had more compliments on my music collections when I've included library tracks than I can count.

décor

Creating the right atmosphere for your shindig is all-important. This can be as simple as giving your home a thorough cleaning and pulling out the good crystal. But some parties require something more—a touch of glamour, a soupçon of whimsy. Parties thrive on the beautiful and unexpected. I discourage festooning one's home with crepe paper, as it tends to give the impression that you're celebrating a child's birthday (unless, of course, that's what you're doing, in which case it's perfectly acceptable—festoon away). Lots of different things can be done to put the festive in the festivities. Creative crafters can make beautiful items that bring life to the room. The first (and sometimes only necessary) element to a lovely party room, however, is flowers. Think of how important flowers are to a wedding; they help define the event. It's the same for your party. Different sorts of flowers create different sorts of moods. Daisies are very casual and relaxed, whereas calla lilies are much more formal. Choose your flowers as you would your clothing for the party; look for flowers that put you in the mood you want to set. Most cities have wholesale flower markets—I suggest exploring them when it comes time to shop for your arrangements rather than haunting the supermarket flower aisles. The selection is much better; the flowers will be extremely fresh and will come in a more impressive quantity. You should be able to buy them without a resale number if you pay cash.

what to do about smoking

We don't want to squelch our guests' enjoyment of the party by asking them not to smoke, but we also don't want to drive off our other guests with smoke-filled rooms. Is there a happy medium? Well, there are a couple of possibilities.

Fill bowls or goblets with white wine vinegar and set them unobtrusively around your home; they will soak up that smoke smell like nobody's business. (I like to float an artificial flower on the surface so they won't be mistaken for beverages, as happened to my friend Mary Ellen at one of my parties.)

The other way to remove that smoke smell is to set a tin pan on the stove over very low heat and put a few grains of spices like cinnamon or nutmeg in it. Keeping a close eye on the pan, slowly burn the spices away. It will fill your home with a lovely scent and chase that mean old smoke odor away.

the dinner-party centerpiece

The end use of this arrangement dictates several factors, the most important of which is height or, rather, lack of it. You don't want to block the view across the table because it can fragment your guests' conversations in an awkward and arbitrary way. For this arrangement you'll need a low dish or bowl. It can be a feature, or you can completely hide it with foliage. You'll also need Oasis floral foam, flowers of your choice, and filler (greenery, baby's breath, or other plant matter to camouflage the Oasis). You might also need a pencil, to make holes in the Oasis for more delicate stems.

This arrangement depends on the size and shape of the table it will be featured on and how much space you need for serving pieces. Once you've estimated that (by setting out the pieces required on the table along with the place settings), you can start arranging flowers. After shaping your Oasis to fit your vessel, soak the Oasis in water. It's a fascinating product—it will absorb four times its weight in water, which, when your flowers are inserted in it, will keep them fresh. Place the Oasis in the bowl and then build your arrangement from the tabletop up. Start by filling in the perimeter of the Oasis with greenery. Once you've created a "base" for your arrangement, you can start adding flowers. It's important to consider symmetry in an arrangement for a dining table, because it will be viewed in the round. Maintaining symmetry is easier if you work on both sides of the arrangement at the same time. Once you've finished building your centerpiece, put it in place and sit down at the table to test the sight line for guests sitting across from each other. If necessary, reduce the height of your taller flowers.

the buffet centerpiece

This arrangement can be much more grand than the one on your dining table because of the nature of a buffet table or counter. I like to serve at my living room counter and put my floral arrangement in the corner as a visual anchor. The vessel (or vessels) for this arrangement can be much more vertically oriented. We've used three different vases, all at different heights—three is the magic number for an arrangement featuring informal balance, as this one does. For this you can select all sorts of flowers, including large branches, which can be extremely dramatic and beautiful. We've used calla lilies, tulips, and hydrangeas. You'll notice (opposite) that some of the flowers are simply laid on the table as though they are waiting to be put in a vase. This can be done for the evening if you use floral picks—hollow plastic tubes that can be filled with water and have slit caps for inserting the flower. You can then cover the picks with drapery, greenery, or any other 'ery you might have handy.

accent arrangements

These arrangements can be scattered around your home to provide a touch of life to otherwise ordinary tableaux—the bathroom, the foyer, even the kitchen will benefit. These arrangements should be of approximately the same scale as the objects they'll be among. You can make the same arrangement several times for several different locations or vary it for each location using similar flowers. The one on page 60 is made with daisies, one of my favorite flowers and guaranteed not to break the bank. It's very simple. Start with a bowl and create a grid over the top of it using ordinary adhesive tape. Then fill the bowl with fresh water (taking care not to get the edge, where the tape is attached, wet) and start to arrange

your daisies. You want to create a tuffet effect. Start around the edges, then build the dome up. I put this arrangement in my bathroom when I'm entertaining.

Once you've gotten your flowers planned out, you can think about other decorations. What follows are two projects that make wonderful party decorations. They can also be used as hostess gifts or be given to a guest of honor.

stained glass without the fuss

Plexiglas is a wonderful medium. You're not only working with color and shape, you're also working with light. It comes in a wide range of colors and can be cut into almost any shape imaginable. I suggest having your plastics dealer or craft shop cut the sheets for you if you want to work with unconventional shapes. This one is done with squares and rectangles that are available precut.

You'll need:

> *One 2-by-3-foot rectangle of clear Plexiglas*
> *Smaller rectangles and squares of Plexiglas in various colors*
> *Methylene chloride (a bonding agent, available where you buy your Plexiglass)*

Working in a well-ventilated area (the methylene chloride you'll be using can be noxious), place your bottommost layer (the large clear rectangle) down across two sawhorses and put a light source under it (you may need to support all four edges to keep the piece from bending). Lay out your collage of shapes on the large rectangle, exploring the different effects you get with color when the light shines through them. Once you've achieved a pleasing composition, you can bond the shapes to the base. Remove all but the bottommost shape from your background (you may want to photograph the composition with a digital camera so you remember the order). Methylene chloride bonds Plexiglas instantly, so be sure of your positioning before applying the solvent. Hold your shape down and run the needle tip of the applicator along the crack between the two pieces. Continue until all pieces are bonded to the background. This can be hung in a window, as a room divider, at the back of the buffet table, or just below a ceiling fixture to create a mood for the party. You can make more than one in different sizes and use them together or scatter them around your home to create a theme.

feltcraft—a softer, fuzzier collage

Felt is an easy medium to work with and one of my favorites for crafting. I like to use wool felt. It's much nicer than its synthetic counterparts. You can purchase wool and wool-blend felts from various websites and catalogs, such as A Child's Dream Come True (www.achildsdream.com).

You'll need:

Several felt circles and ovals in ivory
Colored felt pieces
Scissors
Fabric glue or a sewing machine and thread

Cut shapes that please you—circles, hearts, flowers—out of the colored felt pieces and lay them out on the white ovals (we're making a sun). You can overlap them, make mosaics, or lay them out in organized patterns—whatever pleases you and fits the mood or theme of your party. Once you have your composition done, you can glue or stitch them down. If you're feeling really ambitious, you can embellish them with embroidery. Depending on the size of your finished pieces, you can use them as hot pads on the buffet table, wall hangings, coasters, or place cards. Once the party is over, you might even want to sew backs on them and make them into pillows.

games

Party games, once the darling of the middle class, have gone out of fashion, and I think it's a shame. They're a wonderful way for people to get to know each other. They involve your entire gathering in an activity, so even wallflowers can enjoy what they so frequently miss if no organized activity is planned. There are lots of games that don't require much equipment or preparation. The most famous is, of course, charades. If you're unaware of the premise, you divide the party up into two teams. Each team comes up with a list of book titles, movie titles, television show titles, and the like, writes them on separate slips of paper, and puts them into a hat. Then a member of one team pulls a title out of the opposing team's hat and has to act it out for his team without sound. If the team members guess the title, they win; if they don't, they lose.

Another game that my graphic designer Tamar told me about is hilarious as well. Everyone sits in a circle, then the host takes a dictionary, opens it to a random page, and finds an obscure word that nobody knows the meaning of. The guests (who have been given paper and pencil) make up a definition for that word. Afterward, you go around the circle and each person reads their definition. Finally, the host reads the real one and passes the dictionary on to the next person, who chooses the next word. It's an uproarious game, with lots of funny definitions being read.

Julia Van Vliet, one of the members of my art department, has another game that's an awful lot of fun. She calls it "Who's in Your Bag." This game is best played among close friends, because it requires knowing your playing partners. The object is to liken the people you're playing with to public figures, creating a "bag" full of people who remind you of the person. Say your friend Burt reminds you of Bobby Trendy, looks a little like Abe Vigoda, and, because of his name, makes you think of Bert from Sesame Street. All of those people would then go into his "bag." Sitting in a circle, each person gets a turn at being defined. It can be fun and eye-opening at the same time. It's best not to play this game if there is any animosity in the room at the time, however.

board games

Board games can be a delightful diversion. I like to keep a few on hand to bring out if my party has a bit of a lull. To make it fun, why not make your own boards out of felt using the method described in the décor section of this chapter (page 62) Many different games lend themselves to felt boards, including Parcheesi, checkers, and chess.

card games

One of the tried-and-true American traditions is poker or bridge night. It's a chance for friends to get together regularly and talk about the events of the week, and a wonderful way to break the ice when getting to know new people. Having regular card parties is not complicated, but you might want to invest in a few items to make occasions more special. Vintage versions of card-playing accessories are highly collectible and can be found on auction sites, in vintage stores and thrift shops, and even at department and specialty shops that feature vintage reproductions. I like to have on hand a folding card table, a couple of sets of fun vintage playing cards, and a poker chip dispenser and chips. If you really want to explore the genre, look into getting a bridge set (plates and cups sold in sets of four that were designed specifically for card parties).

party tipples, nibbles & spreads

What would an affair be without refreshments? Pretty darn boring, I'd say. Part of the joy of attending a party is the food and drink that's there waiting for you. And part of the joy of giving a party should be creating, curating, and culling that collection of coveted cuisine. How you present and serve everything is almost as important as the food itself. It's important to assemble a good collection of serving pieces that will supply your guests with the eats as well as look pretty. I like haunting thrift shops and flea markets for such things (as I do for just about everything else). Objects to consider acquiring are a chafing dish, a cake plate, a cheese board, buffet servers, various trays and presentation platters, serving utensils, and, if you have the storage space, specialty items like a deviled egg platter. These items are part of the hostess's kit and represent her to her guests as much as her home; therefore, they should coordinate with the style of the home they're used in. These items are so much fun to hunt for and, unless they break, need only be bought once, so collect the tools of your trade and you're ready to go!

stocking your bar

Your bar requires some very specific equipment, and the more of it you have the more established a host, you'll appear to be. First and foremost on your list should be a mixing glass and glass stirring rod, or a shaker, preferably both. They are used for creating those mixed drinks that are the cornerstone of any bartender's repertoire, as well as the flights of fancy that are so much fun to make.

You'll also want bar spoons for removing olives, cherries, and onions from their respective jars; a bottle opener; a corkscrew; an ice bucket and a pair of tongs; and, last but not least, a jigger measure. Optional equipment can include a soda siphon, bar napkins, and a cocktail recipe book.

It's also important to think about glasses for your drinks—Not that you need all the different kinds. For liquor and cocktails served on the rocks (on ice), highball glasses (middle-height glasses) can substitute for tall, thin Collins glasses and the classic, squat old-fashioned glasses. Tumblers (taller versions of highballs) will work too. For mixed drinks served neat (no ice), you'll want some sort of cocktail glasses (stemmed so as not to transfer the heat of your hand to the drink).

Now, for your ingredients, you'll want to start with the fixings for a popular drink—I suggest something like the martini. For this you'll need to stock vermouth, vodka, and gin (it's best to have both vodka and gin so you can satisfy everyone's preferences). I would then suggest adding things like rum, rye, bourbon, and a bottle of Angostura bitters. Your next additions should be a good bottle of scotch, then sherry. After that it becomes a free-for-all. There are all sorts of liquors, liqueurs, and other exotic ingredients out there waiting to be discovered. Add whatever strikes your fancy; don't be afraid to experiment.

Now, let's talk about those drinks: What will we serve from the bar? I have a few suggestions. Personally, I like champagne. The champagne cocktail has gotten a bad rap in recent years, but I think it's time for a revival. Champagne is not necessarily something to keep on hand in your bar. It should be bought for the occasion. Here are a few drinks that use champagne to its best advantage.

the classic champagne cocktail

You'll need:

1 sugar cube
1 whole lemon
1 small piece of ice
Dash of Angostura bitters
Champagne (the best you can afford), chilled
Lemon peel curl

Begin by rubbing the sugar cube against the outside of a plump lemon, getting as much oil from the zest (lemon peel) as possible on the cube. Then place the cube in the bottom of a lovely champagne glass, along with a small piece of ice and the bitters. Fill the glass with champagne and stir once or twice. Garnish with the lemon peel curl.

Serves 1

bowl or flute?

The champagne bowl derives, as legend has it, from the shape of Marie Antoinette's breast. It's a very elegant shape and was popular in the '50s and '60s. The flute, however, is supposedly the more appropriate glass to serve champagne in because there is a much narrower opening for the bubbles to escape from, thereby keeping the carbonation in the wine, not releasing it into the atmosphere. When it comes right down to it, either glass is usually so small that (at least with my guests) the champagne doesn't have enough time to breathe, let alone release a significant portion of its carbonation before it's been gulped down. So the style of glass you choose really depends on what you find most attractive. I would, however, avoid serving it in the two-piece plastic champagne glasses, unless you are hosting a party of 150 or more. We don't want to be perceived as cheap, now, do we?

the air mail

This is a rich, wintry cocktail with honey and rum.

You'll need:

Juice of ½ lime
1 teaspoon honey
1½ ounces Bacardi Limon
Cracked ice
Dry champagne, chilled

In your cocktail shaker, combine the lime juice, honey, and rum and shake. Add the cracked ice and shake again. Strain the contents into a cocktail glass and fill with champagne.

Serves 1

the peach velvet

This one is lots of fun. It originated at the now-demolished Savoy-Plaza in New York and is almost more like a dessert than a drink.

You'll need:

1 peach, peeled and sliced
4 pieces cracked ice
Dash of peach brandy
Champagne, chilled

Arrange the peach slices attractively in a bowl-type champagne glass. Then add the remaining ingredients and serve to your delighted guest.

Serves 1

schussboomer's delight

From the Sun Valley Lodge in Idaho, the Land of Potatoes, we can enjoy the Schussboomer's Delight.

You'll need:

> *2 ice cubes*
> *¾ ounce fresh lemon juice*
> *1½ ounces cognac*
> *Champagne, chilled*

Stir the ice, lemon juice, and cognac together in a Collins glass, then fill with champagne.

Serves 1

Hint: Incidentally, don't greet a guest at the door or see a guest off with a drink in your hand. It's considered gauche.

Let's not forget those teetotalers out there. If you're having a party with more than four guests, there'll likely be someone who doesn't drink. Here are a few drinks to have on hand for them.

lemonade...from scratch

This simple, refreshing drink really is easy to make and much better than a mix. By the way, these measurements are approximate. Adjust the recipe to your own taste, whether that's on the sweet or the tart end of the spectrum. You can also perk this up for your drinking friends with a dash of Bacardi Limon.

You'll need:

2¼ cups sugar
½ cup fresh lemon juice
¾ teaspoon salt
Fresh mint leaves, for garnish

Combine 6 cups water and the sugar in a saucepan, bring to a boil, and simmer for 2 minutes. Remove from the heat and chill in the fridge. When fully chilled, add the lemon juice and salt. Serve with fresh mint leaves.

Serves 6

teetotaler's glög

For cold-weather gatherings you might want something a little heartier. Should one of your drinking guests be a bit envious of this concoction, you can replace the cider with mulled wine, rum, or brandy.

You'll need:

4 teaspoons molasses
4 tablespoons strained fresh lemon juice
6 ounces apple cider
3 cups hot tea or water
Ground nutmeg
4 cinnamon sticks

Put the molasses, lemon juice, and cider in a pitcher, then add the tea or water and stir well. Pour into mugs, sprinkle with nutmeg, and add a cinnamon stick to each.

Serves 4

fun with balls

Cocktail parties require your guests to be physically adept. Juggling food and a drink is never an easy task, so I suggest giving them nibbles that are hearty and delicious but most of all ambulatory. (No, I don't mean the food should follow your guests around on its own; rather, the nibbles should be easy to tote with a minimum of hands.)

Bite-sized morsels are perfect for cocktail party guests. They can be served on toothpicks and are easy to manage with one of those cocktails in your hand. On the following pages, you'll find some delicious recipes that will have your guests oohing and aahing over your culinary expertise.

ham & egg balls — they're not just for breakfast anymore

These morsels utilize the breakfast staples of ham and eggs in an entirely new way. The result is a rich, sophisticated concoction that defies definition.

You'll need:

3 hard-boiled eggs
1/2 teaspoon chopped fresh chives
1 1/2 tablespoons mayonnaise
Salt to taste
Paprika to taste
1/4 pound lean cooked ham
1/4 cup crushed nuts or corn flakes

Shell and separate the eggs and mash the yolks with a fork in a small bowl until smooth. Add the chives and mayonnaise and season with salt and paprika. Puree the whites in a food processor with the ham until finely ground, then add to the yolk paste. Don't be afraid to add a bit more mayonnaise at this point; the goal is to maintain a smooth consistency. Roll the mixture into balls about 1 inch in diameter and then roll the balls in the nuts (for an extremely rich concoction) or crushed corn flakes (for a lighter result). Serve with toothpicks.

Makes about 20 balls

green balls

These owe their leafy, fresh appearance to the herbs they're rolled in.

You'll need:

> *3 ounces cream cheese*
> *½ cup grated Swiss cheese*
> *Dash of salt*
> *Dash of pepper*
> *Dash of dry mustard*
> *Minced fresh herbs*

Combine all the ingredients (except the herbs) in a bowl and mix with a fork until well blended. Form into ¾-inch balls and roll the balls in the herbs.

Makes about 24 balls

burning bush

These tasty treats are named for the flaming red color of the minced dried beef.

You'll need:

> *3 ounces cream cheese*
> *½ teaspoon minced onion*
> *Minced dried beef*

Combine the cream cheese and onion in a small bowl with a fork until well blended. Form into ¾-inch balls and roll the balls in the dried beef.

Makes about 20 balls

Other balls can be made with soft cheeses and herbs, meats, or nuts. Use your imagination. Try exotic cheeses and your favorite solid ingredients to make delicious new taste sensations. Keep your guests guessing, and your balls could be a real conversation piece!

beef à la lyndstrom a.k.a. köttbullar or swedish meatballs

No discussion of balls would be complete without talking about Swedish meatballs. This is a wonderful dish for entertaining. They're quite elegant served on toothpicks out of a chafing dish. This is one of my favorite recipes.

You'll need:

¼ cup (½ stick) butter
3 tablespoons minced onion
one 1-inch-thick slice of bread
½ cup milk
½ pound ground beef
¼ pound ground pork
¼ pound ground veal
1 egg
1 teaspoon salt
⅛ teaspoon pepper
½ teaspoon ground nutmeg
½ teaspoon sugar
1 tablespoon flour
½ cup beef stock, warmed
1 cup cream or milk, warmed

Melt 1 tablespoon of the butter in a sauté pan over medium heat and cook the onion until lightly browned. Soak the bread in the milk until soft. Combine all the remaining ingredients except the flour, stock, and cream, and mix well with your hands. Use your hands; nothing else will combine the ingredients as well. Then roll the meat mixture into small balls and brown them in the rest of the butter.

Remove the meatballs from the pan and set them aside. Pour off all but 3 tablespoons of the fat from the pan. Add the flour and stir until it's mixed well with the fat. Remove the pan from the heat, then add the stock and cream. Stir constantly until the gravy is smooth and has thickened. Put the meatballs back in the pan with the gravy and cover.

Simmer over very low heat for 30 minutes to 1 hour, then transfer to a chafing dish and serve.

Makes 25–30 balls

deviled eggs — also known as oblong heaven

I like to serve these at afternoon get-togethers in the summer. If I could subsist on them eggclusively, I just might!

You'll need:

> *12 hard-boiled eggs, cooled completely*
> *2 tablespoons mayonnaise*
> *1 tablespoon white vinegar*
> *1 teaspoon dry mustard*
> *1½ teaspoons Worcestershire sauce*
> *¾ teaspoon salt*
> *⅛ teaspoon pepper*
> *⅛ teaspoon paprika*
> *¼ cup grated sharp cheddar cheese*
> *Chopped fresh chives, for garnish*

shelling eggs

Getting those hard-boiled eggs out of the shell can be quite a chore. I've found that the best way begins with the cooking. Boil your eggs for exactly ten minutes, then transfer them to a bowl of cold water immediately and leave them there for at least another ten minutes. This will stop the cooking of the eggs and ensure the easy removal of the shells. Once your eggs have cooled, take one and crack the shell, starting at the large end, where the little pocket of air usually is, and continue all the way around. Then, under running water, find or make a small tear in the membrane beneath the shell and let the water run between the membrane and the egg. The water will do most of the work for you and the egg will practically peel itself!

Shell the eggs, cut them in half lengthwise, and remove the yolks carefully. (We don't want messy broken whites, do we?) Put the yolks in a bowl and mash with a fork. Add all the remaining ingredients (except the chives) to the yolks and mix well. Place a dollop of the yolk mixture in the indentation in each of the egg white halves and garnish with chopped chives.

Here's a hint: Cut your chives up with scissors instead of a knife. The process will go much more quickly.

Makes 24 pieces

finger food topiary

This fun idea is perfect for serving the hors d'oeuvre balls featured on pages 73 through 75. Buy Styrofoam spheres, wooden dowels, papier-mâché flowerpots, and plaster of Paris. Stand one dowel upright in each flowerpot and fill it about a quarter of the way with the plaster of Paris. Let set up and then top each dowel with a Styrofoam orb or two. You can then decorate the dowel with paint and ribbon and the pot with ribbon, doilies, tissue paper, or netting and pompons. Cover the Styrofoam ball with leaf lettuce by pinning the leaves on with straight pins. Then stick the hors d'oeuvre balls into the foam with toothpicks and let your guests pluck them from the "topiary" that results. (See the photo on page 72.)

rewards for the clean plate club

For dessert for your ravenous hordes, try preparing some easy-to-handle homemade candies.

candied citrus rind

This old-fashioned favorite can be made chic by an elegant presentation: Display them upright in a glass or fanned out on a dish, garnished with edible flowers.

You'll need:

Rinds of 2 large grapefruits or 3 large oranges
1 teaspoon salt
2 cups sugar, plus additional for dredging

Fill a bowl with enough hot water to cover the rinds, stir in the salt, and let the rinds soak overnight. The next day, drain the rinds and cut them into long strips. The longer the strip, the more elegant they'll look and the easier they'll be to handle. Combine the sugar and 1 cup water in a saucepan over low heat and cook until the sugar is dissolved. Simmer the rinds in the simple syrup until they take on a translucent, candied appearance. Spread a layer of sugar on wax paper, dredge the rinds in the sugar, and let them harden.

Hint: If the peels remain limp after they've cooled, boil them for a few more minutes and then dredge them in sugar again.

Makes 25–40 pieces

chocolate-covered pretzel sticks

The combination of salty and sweet here is irresistible; this confection satisfies the yin/yang of snacky cravings perfectly.

You'll need:

Butter, for cooling surface
Colored sugars, nonpareils, crushed nuts, cake decorations (4 cups total)
1 pound chocolate of your choice, chopped (about 4 cups)
50 slim pretzel sticks, the longer the better (about two 8-ounce packages)

Butter a smooth surface—ideally a marble slab (a baking sheet will also do). Place each of the toppings on a separate plate. Using a double boiler or a stainless steel bowl set over a pan of simmering water, melt the chocolate (using a double boiler or the equivalent ensures that we don't burn our chocolate—make sure the water in the lower pan is simmering, not boiling). Keep the heat very low to keep the chocolate pourable as you work. Dip the pretzel sticks in the chocolate, leaving about an inch at the top un-dipped. (Hint: You may have to hold them diagonally to cover them that deeply. If necessary, dip the pretzels a second time or spoon chocolate over the pretzels to get a thicker chocolate coating.) Customize the pretzels by rolling them in colored sugars, crushed nuts (my favorite is pistachio), or cake decorations immediately after dipping them the last time. Lay them out on the buttered surface to cool and harden (this takes about 1 hour; you can speed things up by putting the pretzels in the fridge until the chocolate is set). You'll have delightful chocolate-covered pretzels with built-in handles (the undipped portion of the stick), just perfect for easy nibbling. Display them in glasses with the handles sticking up.

Makes 50 pretzel sticks

serving buffet style

When you're serving your meal from a buffet table it's important to arrange the table to accommodate your guests. We don't want to create traffic jams, now, do we? Is your table against the wall? Then start your guests at one end with the plates, lay out the main and side dishes along the front, and put the flatware and napkins on the other end. If your table is accessible from all sides, start your guests in one corner with the plates; let the food flow around the table and back to the fourth corner, where they can pick up their flatware and napkins.

have a seat, dinner is served

Now, if you're having a sit-down dinner (and preparing it yourself), the key to success is creating things that can be either prepped in advance or made quickly.

simple salad, scintillating salad

This salad uses store-bought mesclun (a mix of young lettuces), which is one of the hostess's best allies. It's made particularly special when you add smoked salmon. You can cut up the salmon and prepare the dressing in advance. All you have to do to serve is toss the ingredients together with the dressing before bringing it to the table in your beautiful salad bowl.

You'll need:

4 cups mesclun
1 cup black olives
½ pound smoked salmon, cut into strips

Combine all the ingredients in a large salad bowl.

Dressing:

1 ripe avocado, peeled and cut into chunks
2 ounces blue cheese, crumbled
3 tablespoons fresh lemon juice
¾ cup olive oil
½ teaspoon salt
½ teaspoon dry mustard
Dash of Angostura bitters

Combine all the dressing ingredients in your blender or food processor and blend until smooth. Just before serving, toss with the salad.

Serves 4

how much to allot per person?

Shopping for your meal can be perplexing. How much do you buy for each guest? Here's a simple chart:

✳

Hors d'oeuvres: For 12 people, 80 pieces if serving before dinner; 125 pieces if serving alone

✳

Wine: ½ to ¾ bottle per person
(a bottle of wine contains about 6 glasses)

✳

Meats, vegetables, potatoes:
Roughly ⅓ pound per person

✳

Pastas and rice (dry):
Roughly 2 ounces per person as a side dish,
4 ounces as a main dish

✳

Dessert: Roughly ¼ pound per person

phoebe's phish

This main-course dish is a recipe from a family friend: Phoebe Carnovsky. It's quick and easy and will win raves. Because the almonds can be prepared beforehand and you can put the liquid ingredients in your frying pan before your guests arrive, you can really cut down kitchen time. I like to serve it with asparagus and jasmine rice. Its flavor is very sophisticated and is wonderful with your favorite white wine.

You'll need:

1 tablespoon butter
1 cup slivered almonds
1 cube or 1 teaspoon liquid concentrate chicken bouillon
½ cup white wine
Dash of lemon juice
4 fillets flounder or sole (about 1⅓ pounds total)
2 tablespoons chopped fresh parsley

In a pan over medium heat, melt the butter and sauté the almonds until they're golden brown. Watch them closely—they like to burn easily. Once they're done, set them aside. (This step can be done in advance; quickly reheat the almonds when you're ready to serve.) Put 1½ cups water in a good-sized frying pan and add the bouillon. Heat until the bouillon dissolves, then add the wine and lemon juice. Bring the liquid to a boil and add the fish. It cooks very quickly, so you can turn it about 1 minute after it's been put in the pan. Remove it when it flakes, about 2 to 3 minutes. Arrange the fish on plates, sprinkle with the almonds and parsley, and serve.

Serves 4

pineapple granita

Pineapple is the international symbol of welcome, and this light dessert is prepared in advance so all you have to do when guests arrive is serve it. I first had it at the beach. It originated with my friend David Mandel, and he's made many variations of it with different fruits.

You'll need:

1 cup sugar
1 pineapple
Fresh berries of your choice, for garnish
Mint leaves, for garnish

Place the sugar and ½ cup water in a saucepan and heat until the sugar dissolves into a clear liquid (simple syrup). Set aside to cool. Cut the pineapple into chunks, discarding the skin and core. Put some pineapple and some simple syrup in a blender or food processor and puree. Repeat until you've pureed all the pineapple and syrup. Pour into an 8- or 9-inch baking pan and freeze partway, stirring occasionally (so it doesn't become too solid to dish up). Scoop the partially frozen mixture into a tub or compote dishes to freeze up completely; it should be somewhat granular and scrape off the pan in long strips with the spoon. Serve garnished with the berries and the mint.

Serves 6

coffee ends the night right

A gracious end to a gracious meal usually involves coffee. Making the perfect cup of coffee is not difficult; it's just a matter of knowing the tricks. I like to use a Chemex pot. It's a beautiful Pyrex glass pot that looks a little like an hourglass. It takes big round paper filters that you fold into a cone and place in the top, then you pour hot water through the grounds in the filter and the coffee drips through to the pot below. It's a "stone-age" version of today's drip coffee pots, but it makes wonderful coffee. The ratio I use is one scoop (or tablespoon) of coffee for each cup desired and one for the pot. This creates a rich brew that satisfies most coffee aficionados.

There's been a lot of talk lately about lattes, espresso machines, and cappuccino. At your next affair, why not serve something a little more exotic: Turkish coffee. It's been around for centuries and makes for a nice alternative to the more mundane brews. You can find Turkish coffee in gourmet stores and stores that sell ethnic groceries. It should be ground very fine to create a rich black beverage that should be served with sweets. In some cultures, it's sipped through a sugar cube held between the teeth. It can be prepared the same way you prepare regular coffee or you can prepare it in a Turkish pot with the traditional heating and reheating method, pouring only the froth from the surface into the cup. Either way, it should be served in *demitasse*: small porcelain cups that hold about two ounces. An old Turkish proverb, "Coffee should be black as hell, strong as death, and sweet as love," probably best describes what your guests should expect from Turkish coffee. They will be delighted at the rich, exotic flavor, and it will provide a very satisfying end to a successful party.

travel

Travel is much more than getting from point A to point B; it should be an adventure! Travel means different things to different people, depending on whether it's compulsory or not. For me, it's a little of both. I love to travel for fun but find business travel tiring. There are many ways to streamline your travel experience and some basic things to consider when contemplating jetting off into the wild blue yonder. In the following pages, you'll find some of my tips and tricks for making your trip tip top.

before you go

Having a rough framework for your travel experience will ensure smooth sailing, while still allowing room for spontaneity.

partners in crime

As far as I'm concerned, your travel companion is the single most important factor of the trip. Picking the right person is indispensable to having a good time. Similar temperaments are important; however, a little variation in interests can provide impetus to explore what you might have missed alone. Plan your trip together. Good communication skills are the foundation for a successful trip.

packing

Personally, I don't like to travel heavy. I prefer not to check items if I don't have to, so I economize on space and weight when packing for a trip. The first step to positive packing is selecting the proper wardrobe. Obviously packing for warmer climates is less cumbersome than for colder environments. Whatever your weather expectation, pulling together a look can be easier than you think. I like to base my travel ensembles on a suit. The jacket can be worn with pants, skirt, or dress; or the pants or skirt can be worn with one of several blouses or sweaters, and right there you have nine or ten outfits. Add a dressy blouse that coordinates with the rest and you're set with seven pieces of clothing, at least three of which you'll be wearing to travel in.

Once you've gotten all your clothing pulled together, you need to consider your accessories, toiletries, and what to put it all in. I'm a big fan of the organized travel kit for toiletries. Many suitcases now come with one, which is nice, because it's designed to fit neatly into the bag, taking up a minimum of space. When filling it, consider buying travel sizes of everything you need, and don't take anything that will be provided for you when you get to your destination. I never take shampoo and conditioner anymore because I know there'll be small containers of it waiting for me in my hotel room when I arrive. I've miniaturized everything I need—my toothbrush, toothpaste, razor, moisturizer, sunblock, contact lens solution, and so forth can all be purchased in sample sizes perfect for travel. If you use brands that aren't available in small sizes, you can usually transfer them to travel-sized containers designed for just that purpose. This makes all the difference in space allocation when you're trying to keep your baggage light. If you have items that you'll need when you get there but would make traveling unnecessarily lugubrious, why not ship them? Yes, the mail service is the traveler's friend! I routinely ship wardrobe out to locations when we're shooting. It cuts down on the frustration of trying to cart it along myself. Likewise, I'm always shipping things back home as well. I frequently buy much more than I could ever carry home from my travels, and it's a great boon to drop it off at a mail shop and have it appear on my doorstep a few days after I return home. Packing is all about planning. The more you consider what you'll need, the less you'll be saddled with as you volley from pillar to post.

Wherever you go,
there you are, so why
not look your best?

countdown to fun—keep a travel checklist

I like to keep a checklist on my computer to remind me what basics I need to bring along on my trips. All I need to do is print it out when I'm packing to be sure I'm not forgetting anything. Life is so much easier when it's all mapped out for you! Here's my checklist:

Toothbrush and toothpaste
Floss
Razor
Moisturizer
Contact lenses, case, and solution
Brush
Curling iron
Makeup kit
Underwear for X days
2 pairs of hose
Watch
Sunglasses
Computer
Power cord for computer
iPod, earphones, iTrip, power cord, and car adapter
Book
Cell phone and power cord
Daily planner
Trip information (hotel addresses and
telephone numbers, flight information)

keeping body and soul together

How do you manage life's little necessary processes when traveling? It can seem so complicated to sleep enough, eat properly, and stay regular. I like to bring along simple travel snacks that provide a balance between nutrition and taste. They also solve the increasing problem of the lack of food on flights these days.

scramble—for a nosh

Here's my recipe for Scramble. It's quick and easy, and, in addition to being tasty, it's also a good source of fiber. Pack this in small portable containers and bring it along on your trip for a quick fix for your hunger problems.

You'll need:

2 pounds mixed salted nuts
16-ounce package Multi-Bran Chex cereal
10-ounce package Cheerios cereal
6 ounces sesame stix
6 ounces pretzel sticks
6 ounces small pretzel twists
5 ounces Corn Nuts
2 cups salad oil
2 tablespoons Worcestershire sauce
1 tablespoon garlic salt
1 tablespoon seasoned salt

Preheat the oven to 250°F. Mix all the ingredients together in a large pan and bake for 2 hours, stirring gently every 15 minutes.

Makes 9 quarts

For dessert, bring along dried fruit, hard candies, or chews. I caution against chocolate, however. It's temperature-sensitive, and we don't want ugly brown stains on our new travel suit, now, do we?

acclimating ourselves

Getting settled while traveling—whether it's into a rental car, hotel room, or friend's home—can be difficult. No matter what the location or situation, a few simple rules apply.

look around you

It's important to know your surroundings. If you're slipping into a rental car for the first time, take a moment to learn the layout. It will save time and perhaps prevent an accident if you know how to operate everything before you set off on your adventures. The same applies for your living quarters. Get to know not only the location of the hotel or home you're staying in by locating landmarks and noting the direction of the freeway and surrounding roads, but peculiarities of your room as well. How does the entertainment system work? What do the light switches turn on and off? How does the climate control system work? All these questions, if answered by an initial inspection of your room, will streamline your experience tenfold.

unpack

It may be tempting to throw your bags down, strip your clothes off, and run down to the beach immediately after checking in. But if you take a moment to open up your luggage and pull out the clothes that should hang before you impulsively dive in head first, you can save yourself some work. I prefer not to use the drawers provided for me, only the closet. I pull out the luggage rack and open my suitcase up immediately upon checking in, then hang up anything that might otherwise need ironing. It saves quite a bit of time. I then feel free to go enjoy my surroundings.

bidding a fond adieu

When it comes time to leave, I like to pack the night before. It's usually such a rush the next day with an early flight or at least a somewhat early checkout required in most hotels. Putting everything back in your suitcase except for what you'll be wearing and piling all your luggage in an out-of-the-way but accessible location ensures that nothing will be forgotten in a hasty departure.

travel tips

➥ Photograph your luggage and its contents. If it's lost you'll have a record of it for the airline.

➥ Wear a bodysuit instead of a regular blouse on the plane—it won't ride up and come untucked, looking rumpled and feeling untidy.

➡ Print out address labels for all your friends and put them in a bag with stamps and a pen so you're all ready to send out your postcards.

➤ Your toiletry bottles are much less likely to explode with air pressure differences if you squeeze the air out of them before packing them in your luggage.

life's happy milestones

Celebrating important moments is a way to stay in touch with the cycles of life. It grounds us in the great scheme of things and helps us feel as though we matter. There are lots of milestones in our lives, and they all have one thing in common—they're more meaningful and enjoyable when shared with people who are important to us. When it comes down to it, living graciously is about honoring yourself and your friends and family, however you define them. In the following pages, you'll find ideas for gift giving and gatherings that will make your loved ones feel like you love them more than your cat.

gift giving

Giving someone a really meaningful gift is such a satisfying experience. I pay close attention to friends and family when having a conversation. More often than not, you'll get plenty of hints as to what would be the ideal gift. For instance, I remember demonstrating on my show a pair of magnifying make-up glasses with individual lenses that flip up to allow access to the eye. My producer thought these were delightful. I filed that little bit of information away and when her birthday came around, I found her a vintage pair, complete with their original packaging. She couldn't have been more pleased. Gift giving isn't about how much money you can spend, it's how creative you can be with the money you have.

I also like to have gifts on hand to give on the spur of the moment. In my gift bag right now I have a guidebook to New York restaurants from the '30s (perfect for any New Yorkophile with a sense of history), a few lovely vintage scarves, a couple of sets of vintage Swank cufflinks, a darling cocktail shaker, a copy of *Esquire's Handbook for Hosts* from the '70s, a beautiful purple leatherbound blank book, a collection of postcards featuring photographs from vintage catalogs, and a vintage pottery bowl. I can grab any one of those gifts on the way out the door and present them to almost anyone. It's a real time saver.

let's rap about wrap

How your gift is presented is just as important as what it is you're presenting. Creative gift wrap is a wonderful opportunity for self-expression. And there are so many more ways of presenting a gift than just covering it in paper. Here are some clever ideas for wrapping your gifts.

Wallpaper is a fun choice for gift wrap. It can be found in home improvement stores, but I think the more interesting specimens are found at thrift shops and tag sales—that's where you see the vintage patterns that will strike a nostalgic chord with the recipient. When wrapping a gift with wallpaper, it's fun to play with the intended use and decorate the gift with decorative switchplates or outlet plates. Many thrift shops have them in their "junque" drawers. The elaborate filigree, ceramic, or wood veneer kinds are oftentimes beautiful and can add a touch of whimsy. If you find one with two holes you can thread ribbon through them. If it has only one, try catching a decorative bar of some kind under the ribbon to hold it on.

Large gifts can be wrapped in old posters and smaller ones in color copies of photographs. These graphic images make interesting and unexpected wrapping. You can even cut pages out of magazines to use as gift wrap if your gift is small enough.

If you are feeling especially creative, why not make your own gift wrap? This is a wonderful project for children and can be done in a number of different ways. Simply draw on larger sheets of paper with magic markers or crayons—or use rubber stamps or even cross sections of vegetables dipped in paint to create interesting patterns. Sticker collections are also a fun and clever way to decorate a gift.

flowerpot wrap

An ordinary terra-cotta flowerpot is perfect for a smaller gift. After the gift is removed, the pot can be used as a decorative accessory—or even filled with a real plant or flower.

Paint your popsicle stick green, then drill a hole that's just large enough to fit a round toothpick through, about 1/4 inch from one end. Line the pot in brown netting or tulle, put your gift in, and top it off with more tulle. Next, cut a circle out of cardboard and glue your popsicle stick to it, overlapping the circle about 1/2 inch. Cover it with pompons on one or both sides to create a perky flower. (If you prefer, you can cut a tulip shape or a flower with petals out of paper and eschew the pompons for paint.) Cut another circle of the cardboard the same diameter as the inside of the pot about 1 inch below the top edge, then make a slot for the popsicle stick in the center of the circle. Stick the drilled end of the popsicle stick through the slot until the hole is clear and push the toothpick through the hole. Then pull the popsicle stick up until the toothpick is up against the underside of the cardboard. Glue the toothpick to the underside of the cardboard circle with enough glue to keep it from moving around. Decorate the "stem" with paper leaves. Set this unit aside to dry. Once it's dry, wedge the circle in the pot and the gift is ready to give to your delighted guest.

You'll need:

Terra-cotta flowerpot

Popsicle stick

Green paint

Drill and small drill bit

Brown net or tulle

Stiff cardboard

Scissors

Pompons

Glue

Round toothpick

Leaves or green paper to cut leaves from

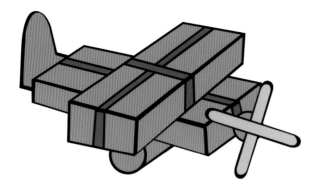

variations on the gift tower

One of the nicest things to receive is the gift tower—a collection of smaller gifts presented as one package. Most of the time gifts are just stacked from largest to smallest from the bottom up. Why not create something a little more whimsical for your honoree? Gifts can be bundled together to create airplanes, automobiles and locomotives, snowmen, or fluffy creatures and birds. Why not create a hot-air balloon with a basket full of small goodies? Let your imagination (and your gifts) lead the way!

gift accents

I like to use accents for simply wrapped gifts. When giving a tie in a recognizable tie box, try tying another tie around the wrapped box. It will fool your recipient into thinking the gift couldn't be a tie because there's already a tie on the box. Depending on the size of the gift, you can also decorate with costume jewelry, cookies or candy, artificial flowers, belts, antique linens, small books, fluffy pom-pons, bells, vintage toys, Christmas ornaments (even if it's not Christmas)—anything that's small and has a clever look to it.

celebrations

Celebrating is a joy! Bringing friends and family together is in itself a reason to celebrate, but when compounded with a special occasion, it's a double delight. There are some occasions that occur in everyone's life, from birthdays and anniversaries to graduations and weddings. All of them have traditional ways to honor them. To make them special we need to transcend the traditional and explore alternative ideas. Thinking outside the gift box is such a fun thing to do when planning a celebration. Why not put a twist on a surprise party and hold it a week early? How about imposing a fun dress code on a fête celebrating one of your own accomplishments by telling guests to wear only black and white, then you come in red? My photographer, Brad, threw a birthday party for a friend at an indoor pool in February. It was delightful to be able to swim in the middle of winter—and what a wonderful gift to his friend to have such an unusual birthday celebration. The important thing is to not limit yourself to the old clichés, but to reinterpret and reinvent them. Making our loved ones feel special is such a splendid way to give of ourselves. It just takes a little thought.

birthday breakfast

Whatever your age, birthdays are a gift. Making the most of them is an obligation. Spending birthdays with the people who are important to us grounds us and makes the tradition of celebrating the anniversary of our birth mean something. Those people frequently wake up under the same roof as we do, so what would be more natural than to have a celebration at the start of the special day?

omelets

There's a cachet to the omelet: People who make them often like the people they make them for to think that only they have the magic touch to create the wondrous dish. But it's just not so. Omelets depend on two things: using a very clean pan and properly preheating it. Your pan must be spotless; any detritus can interfere with the flipping process and adversely affect the taste if you're using delicately flavored ingredients. It must be very hot to ensure that the bottom of the omelet will be nicely cooked while the center remains runny.

The nice thing about an omelet is that it's truly a blank canvas. You can put almost any savory and even a few sweet ingredients in it and be assured that it will be delicious. I like experimenting with cheeses, herbs, meats, and vegetables to create heretofore unheard-of combinations to tempt the tastebuds. Start by putting your eggs in a bowl—you can put all the eggs for everyone's omelets (2 to 4 eggs per person) in one bowl—and beating them. You can add a little milk or water to make the consistency a little more pourable, and a dash of salt and pepper. Then begin preparing your pan. The pan should be about 9 but no more than 10 inches in diameter—a larger pan will create an unwieldy omelet. Heat it until a drop of water beads and bounces in the pan, and then add a tablespoon of butter. Once that's melted, you can put your eggs in. Roll the eggs around the pan until only the center is soft and toss your add-ins onto the soft center. Fold one side over, slide the omelet off onto the plate, and serve! Easier than you thought it would be, isn't it?

flaming fruit kebabs

This eye opening dish is mostly flash and very little substance, but the fresh fruit is delicious and good for the digestion.

You'll need:

> 2 quarts fresh fruit such as pineapple chunks, strawberries,
>   grapes, orange sections, and mango
> 12 soft bread cubes
> 1 bottle lemon extract
> 4 metal kebab skewers

Prepare this dish right before serving. Start by cutting up the fruit into bite-sized pieces (this can be done in advance), then soaking the bread cubes in the lemon extract. Anything soaked in lemon extract will burn with a lovely blue/yellow flame—that includes your clothing, the Formica, and this book, so be careful. Stack the fruit on the skewers, interspersing a cube whereever you'd like a flame. Be sure not to put a bread cube too close to the handle of the skewer. When the kebabs are all stacked, light the bread cubes. They'll burn nicely for a few minutes, but be sure to blow them out before trying to eat the fruit. Also, it's probably not a good idea to serve this dish in bed.

Serves 4

When thinking about a breakfast celebration, cake isn't the first thing that comes to mind. It is, of course, traditional for birthdays, and who as a child hasn't pined for a slice of chocolate cake while sitting at the breakfast table contemplating their oatmeal? The nice thing about a celebration like this is that it comes but once a year, so the inclusion in the menu of a rich, decadent chocolate cake is a welcome and harmless flight of fancy that wields so much more impact then it does as the culmination of an evening meal. On the practical side, a piece of chocolate cake has a similar effect on the subsequent day as drinking a cup of coffee does—the caffeine and sugar wake the body up, and the richness satisfies the soul.

grandma bea's chocolate cake

This is my favorite chocolate cake recipe, but it isn't actually mine. It was given to me by a dear friend, Julie Kurnitz, on one of my television show episodes, and it was her grandmother who originated it. But then, that's how recipes are passed down, isn't it?

You'll need:

½ cup (1 stick) butter
1¾ cups sugar
2 cups flour
6 tablespoons unsweetened cocoa powder
½ teaspoon salt
1 teaspoon baking soda
3 eggs
1 teaspoon vanilla
1 cup sour cream
¼ cup hot water

Preheat the oven to 350°F. In a mixing bowl, cream together your butter and sugar. (Baking recipes always seem to begin with this step, don't they?) Sift all the

cake decorating

Now, a birthday cake should look like a birthday cake, right? Don't be daunted by cake decorating. Keep it simple and your cake will look professionally casual. The mid-century style of cake decorating is very popular today, and it's all about seeing the hand of the decorator in the finished result. Separate your icing into several different dishes and then tint each dish a different color with a little food coloring. You can then put your icing into pastry bags and pipe on simple dots or stripes. Don't feel you need to write a name on the cake. It's difficult to make the letters even and professional looking. If you don't have a pastry bag, you can use a plastic freezer bag. Place some icing in the bag, force it into the corner, and clip off just the very point for small lines or dots; clip a little higher for larger dots or lines. If you don't want to attempt the pastry bag, even just casually scattered nonpareils are a lovely way to say "Happy Birthday" to your nearest and dearest. Don't even feel you have to have candles; they can be an unwelcome reminder of the passage of time.

dry ingredients together into another bowl and set them aside. Add the eggs to the butter and sugar mixture, one at a time, then add the vanilla. Alternate adding the dry ingredients and sour cream in three parts, mixing well after each addition, then the hot water and mix well. Pour into two greased and floured 9-inch round pans. Bake for 30 to 40 minutes, until a toothpick inserted in the center comes out clean. Julie says the cake needs no icing, but we like to gild the lily, don't we? I suggest the following lovely uncooked icing.

Serves 8–10

cream cheese icing

You'll need:

> *One 8-ounce package cream cheese*
> *1½ tablespoons cream or milk*
> *2 cups confectioners' sugar, sifted*
> *1 teaspoon vanilla*
> *½ teaspoon cinnamon*

In a mixing bowl, combine the cream cheese and milk and mix until soft and fluffy. Gradually beat in the confectioners' sugar, and then add the vanilla and cinnamon.

You may have been frustrated in the past when trying to frost a chocolate cake with light-colored icing because the cake crumbs pull up and make dark flecks in your icing. Fear no more. Here's all you need to do: Spread a very thin layer of icing on the cake, letting the crumbs do whatever they want to. Then put the cake in the fridge until the icing sets. Now the crumbs are sealed in and you can add another, thicker layer to your cake without worrying that the result will look dirty.

Makes enough to frost one 9-inch, two-layer cake

summer breeze

This drink is perfect for breakfast celebrations.
It's light and fresh with the tang of citrus.

You'll need:

1½ ounces Bacardi Limon
1 ounce pink grapefruit juice
1 ounce orange juice
Dash of grenadine
1 Maraschino cherry, for garnish

Shake all ingredients (except the cherry) together in a shaker filled with ice. Strain into a martini glass, drop in the cherry, and enjoy!

Serves 1

summer breeze sans spirit

For those of you out there who don't imbibe, here's a nice variation on the Summer Breeze that won't leave you three sheets to the wind.

You'll need:

3 ounces pink grapefruit juice
5 ounces lemon-lime soda
1 orange wheel, for garnish
1 Maraschino cherry, for garnish

Pour the grapefruit juice into a tumbler or highball glass filled with ice cubes and top it off with lemon-lime soda. With a wooden skewer, pierce the orange wheel through both sides of the rind and add the cherry. Add to the drink and serve.

Serves 1

showers

Such traditional wedding events as showers have gotten a black eye since the onset of such dubious new traditions as the "wedding cake in the face" at nuptials. This is ill-deserved, however; the shower is a lovely tradition that can be expanded to include honoring not only brides and new mothers, but new home owners and graduates. The nature of a shower is to help someone amass the necessary objects to achieve some goal—traditionally to set up housekeeping or create a home for a new baby, but it can be reimagined in all kinds of ways. For those who are going out on their own for the first time, gifts like sheets, towels, and pots and pans are always welcome. To celebrate moving to a new home, you could perhaps have a stationery shower with gifts like stationery with the recipients new address on it, personalized memo pads, business cards, and the like.

Showers are traditionally luncheons, with all that implies for the menu. The menu for our shower includes a very mid-century recipe for a Bridge Loaf, so named because it was the perfect thing to serve at card parties. We'll also be serving tea and delightfully rich St. Louis Bars for dessert.

bridge loaf

Special occasions require extra special dishes. This is a complete meal wrapped up in a tidy package that will be remembered by your guests for years to come.

You'll need:

> *1 loaf (1½ pounds) unsliced sandwich bread*
> *½ cup (1 stick) butter or margarine, softened*
> *Shrimp Salad Filling (opposite)*
> *Olive-Nut Spread (opposite)*
> *Deviled Ham Spread (opposite)*
> *Four 8-ounce packages cream cheese, softened*
> *1 cup half-and-half*
> *Few drops of food color, if desired*
> *Vegetable slices, fruit, fresh currants, or herbs for garnish*

Trim the crusts from the bread loaf and cut the loaf horizontally into four equal slices. Lightly spread butter on both sides of the middle two slices, the top of the bottom slice and underside of the top slice. Place the bottom slice on a decorative serving plate, buttered side up, and spread it evenly with some of the Shrimp Salad Filling. Place a double-buttered slice on top of the Shrimp Salad layer. Build your loaf up in this way, using the rest of the bread slices and the Olive-Nut Spread and Deviled Ham Spread, in that order, ending with the top slice (butter side down). Lightly press the loaf together, cleaning up any filling that has oozed from the sides. Stir together the cream cheese, half-and-half, and food color, if using. Spread the mixture over the sides and top of the loaf. Garnish with vegetable slices, fruit, fresh currants, and/or herbs. Refrigerate for about 30 minutes, or until the cream cheese mixture has set. Cover tightly (without making contact with the icing) and refrigerate at least 2½ hours, but no longer than 24 hours. Cut into slices.

Serves 16–20

shrimp salad filling

⅓ cup mayonnaise
¼ cup finely chopped celery stalks
2 tablespoons fresh lemon juice
¼ teaspoon salt
⅛ teaspoon pepper
2 hard-boiled eggs, finely chopped
2 cans (4 ounces each) tiny shrimp, rinsed and drained

Stir all the ingredients together in a small bowl.

olive-nut spread

6 ounces cream cheese, softened
1 cup (4 ounces) finely chopped walnuts
½ cup finely chopped pimiento-stuffed olives
¼ cup milk

Stir all the ingredients together in a small bowl.

deviled ham spread

¼ cup sour cream
¼ cup sweet pickle relish, drained
2 tablespoons grated onion
⅛ teaspoon red pepper sauce
Two 4¼-ounce cans deviled ham

Stir all the ingredients together in a small bowl.

tea suits showers to a t

There's a mystique to tea. In many countries there are age-old rituals and ceremonies surrounding the serving of tea, and my friend Tracy Stern is carrying on
the tradition in New York with her own line of teas and a unique outlook on the
world of tea. She's been hosting tea ceremonies at her salon in the City Club
Hotel for two years now. She says tea is a universal symbol of civility that takes
you out of your everyday run-around existence. The ceremony at her salon
includes experiences for all five senses. It's a way for people to slow down and
connect with each other and themselves. It starts with selecting your blend
from the five Tracy has created; then the tea is put in a press pot with hot
water and allowed to steep for three minutes. During that time you can read
the tea scroll she has provided, which explains what the blends are composed of. Once the three minutes have elapsed, you push down the plunger
and pour the tea. It's presented with a lovely silver tea caddy with rock amber
sugar, warm milk, and honey, as well as cakes and sandwiches decorated
with edible flowers and rose petals.

Tea service like Tracy's is almost spalike in its recuperative effects, and it's
not that difficult to replicate for your shower. Select a blend of tea in advance,

but don't brew it until you're ready to serve it. Have your Bridge Loaf and St. Louis Bars on the table with the tea service and you're ready to serve. Informal service means the hostess pours. For more formal service, have a friend do the honors. Making a fuss can be such fun and so refreshing once in a while, and no one is more worthy of it than our good friends.

st. louis bars

This crowd-pleaser is a combination of cookie and cheesecake. The recipe was given to me by Joe Ligamarri, who came on my show to give me some of his marvelous cookie recipes. It's easy to make and always gets raves.

You'll need:

1 box yellow cake mix
1/2 cup (1 stick) butter, melted
3 eggs
8-ounce package cream cheese
4 1/2 cups confectioners' sugar

Preheat the oven to 350°F. Lightly beat one of the eggs and then, in a mixing bowl, combine it with the cake mix and butter. The mixture will be very stiff. Press it into a 9-by-13-inch pan. Set aside 2 tablespoons of the confectioners' sugar, then, in a food processor or using a hand mixer, combine all the remaining ingredients and process until smooth. Pour this filling over the crust. Bake for 30 to 35 minutes, until the filling does not move when the pan is shaken—it should be a nice golden color. Remove from the oven and sprinkle with the reserved confectioners' sugar. Wait until completely cooled and cut into bars.

Makes 24 bars

family reunions

Family reunions are a wonderful way to celebrate milestones that occur later in life—anniversaries, retirement parties, Grandma's eightieth birthday. Since these are usually outdoor events, here are a few recipes that are perfect for open-air dining.

potato salad

What family reunion would be complete without potato salad? This is my mother's recipe. It's delicious—tasty and tangy, just as potato salad should be.

You'll need:

> 10–12 Red Bliss potatoes, boiled
> (Mom says peel them, but I like them with their peels)
> 6 hard-boiled eggs, shelled
> 3 tablespoons mayonnaise, plus additional if needed
> 1/2 teaspoon curry powder, plus additional to taste
> Salt to taste
> Pepper to taste
> 1/2 cup black olives
> 1/2 cup cocktail olives (reserve 1 tablespoon of the brine)

Cut the potatoes and eggs into small chunks about a 1/2 inch square. Put them in a bowl with the mayonnaise, curry powder, salt, pepper, olives, and reserved brine and mix until well combined. If you find that the ingredients aren't wet enough, you can add more mayonnaise—everything should hold together nicely. Let stand overnight to give the ingredients a chance to marinate. Taste the next day for seasoning. If necessary, add more curry powder, salt, or pepper.

Serves 10–12

almond chicken

This dish is the perfect chicken for meals out-of-doors. It's good both hot and cold and can be eaten with your fingers without making too much of a mess. It also originated with my mother and has always been a crowd-pleaser in our family. These chicken legs make wonderful leftovers, so don't be afraid to overestimate!

You'll need:

24 chicken legs
½ cup flour
¼ teaspoon salt
¼ teaspoon pepper
¼ teaspoon poultry seasoning
6 eggs
2 cups slivered almonds
¼ cup (½ stick) butter, sliced into pats

Preheat the oven to 350°F. Rinse off the chicken legs, then pat them dry. Put the flour, salt, pepper, and poultry seasoning in a plastic bag and then put in two legs at a time and shake them up to coat. Break the eggs into a large, flat bowl or soup plate, add a little water, and beat them together. Dip the floured chicken legs in the egg mixture, and then dredge them in the almonds. Lay the legs out on a greased baking pan and bake for about 25 minutes, or until golden brown and juicy. Dot the chicken with the butter pats halfway through cooking to baste them. Serve immediately or place them in the fridge, covered, overnight and serve cold. Note: If you're not that fond of dark meat, you can make Almond Chicken with two fryers cut into pieces, instead of just legs.

Makes 24 pieces

deep fat frying—the sin worth committing

No kitchen is complete without a deep fat fryer. You can fry almost anything, probably even tofu, and it will be immediately appetizing. Learning the ins and outs of frying can be daunting, however. Here are some tips:

➺ Make sure the temperature of the fat is constant. If the fat gets too hot it will smoke, producing an unpleasant odor; if it's too cool the items won't develop a crust quickly enough and will absorb a lot of the fat and become greasy. Don't attempt to fry without a good frying thermometer and while frying keep it in a glass full of hot water so you don't risk breaking it when dipping it into the hot fat—just be sure to dry it off well before putting it in the fryer.

➽ Fat can be reused: Strain it after each use and store it in the fryer in a cool place, you can reuse it for quite a while. Discard it after it becomes dark and thickens.

➤ When placing food in the fryer, use a pair of metal tongs, a metal spatula, or a slotted spoon that has been dipped in the hot fat so the food will release easily. Some food requires a frying basket.

➽ Don't try to cook too many pieces of food at once—this will lower the temperature of the fat, making for greasy food.

⟹ If your fat should catch on fire, don't panic. Have a lid nearby to stifle the flames. Fat fires can also be put out with salt or baking soda. Never use water—that will only spread the flames. You might consider investing in a multipurpose dry-chemical fire extinguisher. Remember: Prior planning prevents poor performance.

➤ Food to be fried should be as close to room temperature as possible to avoid dropping the temperature of the fat too drastically.

➤ If you're cooking raw foods, they should be dried completely before being put in the fryer. Water will cause the fat to pop and spatter.

homemade doughnuts — always a hole in one

What could be better than homemade doughnuts? Rich and delicious, soft and sweet, they just say "special occasion."

You'll need:

Oil for the fryer
3 eggs
1¼ cups sugar
1 cup sour cream
4 cups sifted flour, plus additional for the work surface
2 teaspoons baking powder
1 teaspoon baking soda
½ teaspoon salt
¼ teaspoon cinnamon

Preheat the oil in a deep-fat fryer to 370°F and line a few plates with paper towels. Beat the eggs in a mixing bowl. Continuing to beat slowly, add the sugar, then stir in the sour cream. In another bowl, resift the flour together with the baking powder, baking soda, salt, and cinnamon. Gradually add the dry ingredients to the egg mixture, stirring until well blended. Dust a work surface liberally with flour and flatten the dough on it, dusting the top with flour as well. Roll out the dough to about ½ inch thick and cut with a doughnut cutter. (If you don't have a doughnut cutter, cut them out with a drinking glass, and make the holes with a shot glass. Or you can make doughnut holes by dropping teaspoons full of dough directly into the fryer.) Reroll the scraps and continue to cut out doughnuts and doughnut holes until you've used all the dough. Fry a few doughnuts at a time until golden brown on the bottoms, then turn and continue to fry until golden brown on the second side, about 1 minute per side. Transfer to the towel-lined plates and let cool slightly. You can sprinkle them with confectioners' sugar or cinnamon sugar, or glaze them with a lovely milk glaze like the one that follows.

Makes about 32 doughnuts and doughnut holes

milk glaze

You'll need:

> 5 tablespoons hot milk
> 1 teaspoon vanilla
> 4 cups confectioners' sugar, sifted

Add the milk and vanilla to the sugar and mix thoroughly to a smooth, pourable consistency. Dunk slightly cooled doughnuts into the glaze, turning to coat them, then transfer them to a wire cooling rack set over a rimmed baking sheet and let the glaze set (this takes just a few minutes).

Makes about 2 cups

Life is all about what you put into it. Take the time to make your days special, and your years will amount to something wonderful. I hope what I've had to say in the preceding pages—both practical and philosophical—has struck a chord with you. I think Patrick Dennis said it best in Auntie Mame—"Live! Live! Live! Life is a banquet and most poor suckers are starving to death!"

bye, now!

index